**Kingdon
Publishe.**

Straightforward Christianity

ISBN: 978-1-913247-08-9

2nd Edition by Kingdom Publishers Kingdom Publishers London, UK.

If you would like to purchase more copies please contact us in the following ways:
Telephone: (+44) 0203 151 0015 Email:
contact@kingdompublishers.co.uk
If you would like to know more about our publishing services please visit our website on http://www.kingdompublishers.co.uk

DEDICATION

For Arthur and Margaret Champion and James
and Jane Howell

Giles
with best wishes
Nigel

CONTENT

Chapter 1 - A founder with universal appeal 1

Chapter 2 - A teaching for everyone 14

Chapter 3 - A Life changing experience 30

Chapter 4 - An exemplary leader to follow 52

Chapter 5 - A present help in suffering 64

Chapter 6 - A way through death 77

Chapter 7 - A future hope 93

Chapter 8 - A straight forward faith 103

Discussion Questions and Topics 117

ACKNOWLEDGMENTS

I am very grateful to my wife, Anne, Rosie Button, Arthur Champion, Jane Howell, Fred Hughes, Cathy Robinson and Martyn Taylor who kindly read the manuscript. They all made a number of helpful suggestions. I am particularly indebted to Maria Yiangou, editor at Kingdom Publishers, for her help and encouragement.

PREFACE

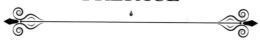

This short book Straightforward Christianity, is written for anyone who wants to know the benefits following Jesus can bring into their lives. I have tried throughout in the chapters that follow this very brief preface to hold to the maxim of John Wesley, one of England's greatest Christian leaders, and write 'plain truth for the plain man [and woman]'. I hope I have succeeded in this objective but you the reader will be the judge!

Nigel Scotland

CHAPTER 1
A Founder with Universal Appeal

Of all the founders of the world's religions Jesus has a universal appeal. This fact is powerfully captured in Salvador Dali's famous painting *Christ of St John of the Cross*. It depicts Jesus with his arms outstretched and looking down over the entire world. The picture demonstrates Jesus' deep compassion and concern for the entire human race. This is the truth so profoundly expressed in John's gospel that 'God so loved the world that he gave us his only begotten son that whoever believes in him should not perish but have everlasting life'.[1] Today the followers of Jesus are numbered in billions and they are found on every continent in the world.

In 1971 two clergymen were standing together on a New York City Street corner and looking up at the billboards outside one of the theatres. One said to the other, 'Do you know that show grossed two million dollars'? The other said: 'Where did we miss out'? The show was Andrew Lloyd Webber's rock opera *Jesus Christ Superstar*! Two million dollars was a huge sum at the time. The show's popularity was testimony to the universal appeal that Jesus still holds for so many in more recent times. This was followed in 1973 by Stephen Schwartz's Broadway musical *Godspell* with a parade of much loved songs including 'Prepare ye the Way of the Lord'. It's not just the musicals which have proved to be so popular, epic films such as Franco Ziffirelli's 1977 *Life of Jesus* were feted in many of the world's countries. Mel Gibson's 2004 *The Passion of the Christ* shattered the box office records.

[1] John 3:16

Jesus' appeal to every race and culture

In Britain, Europe and North America there is a constant media focus on the growing number of multi-racial, multi-ethnic, multicultural societies. Significantly among all the great religious founders Jesus has truly embraced the world's ethnicities and cultures. It is of course good to be reminded that Jesus was Jewish and his skin therefore olive brown. We should however remember that when he poured out his Holy Spirit presence for the very first time on the Day of Pentecost it was a multi-racial event. Among those present in Jerusalem on that occasion there were Jews from Judea, people from Asia, Egypt, Arabia, Rome, Persia and North Africa. Down through the centuries from that day to this very day Jesus' spirit is still impacting the lives of people of every race, colour and culture.

It is also important to recognise that some of the greatest early Christian leaders were Africans. Fast forwarding to the present time we find that Indian Christians think of Jesus as Indian and Indian representations portray him with an Indian face and Indian dress. Indian Christian worship embraces Indian culture and in many places Jesus is often worshipped using Indian percussion drums. Black Christians in America perceive Jesus as black and they worship him with rhythmic joyful dance and wonderful Spirituals. Ethiopian Christians see Jesus as an African and they worship him with African drums, music and dance. People in England think of Jesus as a white man and they mostly worship him in polite and restrained English ways. In the Eastern Orthodox tradition people stand for much of their worship services and they use colourful icons to help them focus on Jesus.

In 1962 Joseph Jobe attempted to bring this Christian diversity together when he wrote *Behold the Man*. It's a survey of the great paintings of Jesus from all the continents of the world. He wrote as follows about the way in which each painter portrayed Jesus in their own culture and ethnicity.

> Each artist has his own language and style in which he has set forth the common faith in the redemption of the world by Our Lord Jesus Christ. So in Asia Christ will be a yellow man, in Africa a black man, also a Bantu among Bantus, or a Madagascan in Madagascar. There is nothing odd in this, since in other times Christ became Roman, Greek, Russian, French, Spanish and German.

Jesus is for everyone because he embraces every race, culture and ethnicity. In his resurrection he was still recognised by his disciples as the same Jesus. Having ascended into the heavens he is still fully human but now honoured and worshipped as the Universal Lord of all, the Saviour for the whole world. This is one reason why there are so many people from so many backgrounds, cultures and colours who follow him in preference to any other.

Jesus' appeal to every social class

From the earliest Christian era there have been people from every social grouping and segment of society who have become committed followers of Jesus. During the time of his earthly ministry a number of wealthy and influential people became his followers. One such was Nicodemus who was a member of the Jewish ruling Council. Another was Joseph of Arimathea who Matthew's gospel describes as 'a rich man'. Three centuries later Constantine was the first Roman Emperor to become a committed Christian. Converted following a vision of the risen Jesus on the eve of the battle of Milvian Bridge in AD 312 he did much to Christianise the Roman Empire. He immediately stopped the persecution of Christians and set about making Christianity a privileged religion. He encouraged the building of public churches and freed clergy from secular work, allowing them to be paid for their pastoral care, teaching and leadership. He strengthened family life and designated Sunday as a day for rest and worship for everyone.

Since Constantine's time there has been a long succession of great Emperors, Kings, Queens and Presidents who have openly followed Jesus. Some who spring to mind are Queen Bertha of Kent, Edward the Confessor, Joan of Arc, King Edward VI, Queen Elizabeth I and Queen Elizabeth II.

Abraham Lincoln, the 16th President of the United States, had a strong awareness of God's hand in the affairs of the American nation and even believed that through the Civil War the divine purposes were being worked out. It was his 'Emancipation Proclamation' which gave freedom to four million slaves. When Jimmy Carter took oath as America's 39th President he used a Bible given to him by his mother instead of the traditional Bible used by every incoming head of state since George Washington in 1789. Jimmy Carter also quoted from the Bible in his inaugural address, 'He hath shown thee, O man, what is good. And what does the Lord require of thee, but to do justly, and to love mercy, and to walk humbly with thy God'

To men such as Constantine, Lincoln and Carter could be added hosts of others from the ranks of the wealthy and the influential who have followed Jesus as their role model and guiding example. William Gladstone, one of Britain's foremost Prime Ministers, was a dedicated and forthright Christian man. Perhaps his personal conviction was never more clearly stated than in an address he once gave to a young people's Bible class. 'Two thoughts I would specially commend to your attentions', he said, 'Christianity is Christ; and nearness to Him and His image is the end of all your effort'. Among hundreds of other national and political leaders with Christian convictions mention could be made of the former Conservative MP and Brexit MEP, Anne Widdecombe, the British Prime Minister Teresa May and Scott Morrison who became Prime Minster of Australia in 2018. Among hundreds of Christian activists the campaigns against slavery led William Wilberforce and Harriet Beecher Stowe, the author of Uncle Tom's Cabin, particularly stand out for me. More recently, Archbishop Desmond Tutu emerged as a vigorous opponent of South Africa's apartheid system and was generous and irenical in his role as Chair of the Truth and Reconciliation Commission when it was finally defeated.

Jesus' appeal to the poor and marginalised

As well as attracting the good and the great Jesus came to hold a special place in the hearts of the poor. He demonstrated God's care and concern for the marginalised, the destitute and the needy. Abraham Lincoln once said: 'God must love the poor because he made so many of them'.[2] Jesus declared that he had come 'to bring good news to the poor'. In his great parable of the Lost Son, Jesus was asserting that every single individual, whether a monarch in a palace or a homeless person on the street, is equally valuable and precious in God's sight. Jesus spent time with those who needed him most - the outcasts, the lepers and those on the margins of society. The very sight of the blind, those who could not walk and the mentally ill who pleaded for his help moved Him with compassion. He reached out with a healing touch to

---

[2] Luke 4:18

the blind who cried out to see, the lame who were desperate to walk and the mentally ill who clamoured for their darkness to be dispelled.

Unsurprisingly the majority of Jesus' followers during the period of his earthly ministry were the poor of the land. They were the hungry he came to feed, the lonely he came to befriend, the guilty who needed forgiveness and the vulnerable he came to protect. On one occasion when Jesus was eating supper in the home of a wealthy man he said to the guests who were sitting at the table, 'When you give a party "call the poor, the blind and the lame"'.[3]

It was Jesus' example of caring for the poor and needy that brought about the founding of hundreds of Christian monasteries. In the Middle Ages the monks cared for the poor, gave them hospitality, provided many with work and prayed and gave them herbal medicines when they were sick. It was through their welcome and compassion that many of the world's early hospitals came to be started.

In eighteenth century England John Wesley, a Church of England clergyman, was so drawn by Jesus, that he left the comfortable surroundings of the Oxford College where he was a tutor, to bring the gospel of Jesus' love and compassion to the needy of England. He preached in the open air, in the fields, on the highways and byways and in the market squares. He called himself 'God's steward of the poor' and on a number of occasions declared, 'I love the poor – in many of them I find pure genuine grace'. In the early days of Methodism Wesley wrote:

Our societies were formed from those who were wandering upon the dark mountains, that belonged to no Christian church, but were awakened by the Methodists, who had pursued them through the wilderness of this

---

[3] Luke 14:13

world to the highways and hedges – to the markets and the fairs – to the hills and dales – who set up the standard of the cross in the streets and lanes of the cities, in the villages, in the barns and farmers' kitchens – and all in such a way, and to such an extent as never had been done before, since the apostolic age.

Wesley's work in converting the poor and promoting education in Sunday schools improved the quality of the lives of Britain's poor. With the passage of time this produced generations of men and women who could read and write. They were then able to stand up for the justice they had learned from the teaching of Jesus and the Old Testament prophets. Some of these men and women emerged as the founders and leaders of the first trade unions. Among them was Tommy Hepburn, a Primitive Methodist local preacher, who organised the first Durham Mine Workers Union. He was renowned for his refusals to begin negotiations with Lord Londonderry and other coal owners in the North East unless they first knelt to pray for God's guidance and justice! Kier Hardie, the Scottish mineworker who founded the Independent Labour Party, was an active practising Christian. Such also was Ben Tillet 'the dock workers' leader who led the famous 'dockers' tanner' strike of 1889 which saw more than 100,000 dock workers obtain a just increase in their pay to six pence a day.

In more recent times many others have been drawn to Jesus on account of his compassion for the poor and been challenged to follow his example. Among some who stand out for this reason are Archbishop Don Helda Camara in Brazil, Archbishop Oscar Romero in El Salvador, Archbishop Trevor Huddleston and Nelson Mandela. Helda Camara will always be remembered for his social and political campaigning on behalf of the poor. Sometimes known 'as the bishop of the slums' he repeatedly spoke out against the injustices of the military dictatorship of 1964-1985. Oscar Romero gave his life in service to the poor. Given the title 'Servant of God' by Pope John Paul II he was martyred in 1980. Trevor Huddleston was a godly anti-apartheid campaigner who was even honoured for his work by the African National Congress. Nelson Mandela was the first black President of South Africa. A life-long opponent of apartheid he was sustained by his Christian faith about which he was outspoken on a number of occasions following his release from prison on 11th February, 1990. Janani Luwum, Archbishop of the Province of Uganda, who is commemorated in Westminster Abbey, stood in opposition to the brutality of Idi Amin and was assassinated for his faith in Christ on 17th February, 1977.

It was Jesus' compassion for the needy that motivated doctors and nurses to invest their lives as Christian missionaries in bringing health care to the suffering peoples of India and Africa. Such was David Livingstone who gave devoted medical aid to the tribal peoples along the banks of Lake Tanganyika. It was Jesus' compassionate spirit in Florence Nightingale that prompted her to travel out to the Crimea to care for the wounded and dying British soldiers. It later led to her founding training schools for nurses. It is the reason that organisations like the Salvation Army spend so much their time working with the homeless and unemployed.

Jesus' appeal to women

Not only was Jesus' appeal to both the rich and the poor, the rulers and the ordinary citizens of the nations, he has also been an inspiration to many millions of women. In particular, women who are treated as outcasts by their culture or society have found affirmation, courage and hope in following Jesus. Sadly, first century Palestine had imbibed earlier Greek attitudes to women as well as those of Roman society. Demosthenes, the C4th BC orator of Athens, had laid it down as an accepted practice among his contemporaries that 'we have courtesans for the sake of pleasure; we have concubines for the sake of daily cohabitation; we have wives for the purpose of having children legitimately, and for having a faithful guardian for all household affairs'. Not only did many of the Greeks at the time of Jesus' earthly ministry hold this low view of women, but their attitudes were shared by many in both Jewish and Roman society.

Every first century male Jew thanked God each day that he hadn't been born a gentile or a woman. Strict first century rabbis were forbidden even to greet a woman in public. No rabbi was ever permitted to speak to his wife, daughter or sister in public. There was even a group of extremist Jewish men who became known as 'The bruised and bleeding Pharisees' because they shut their eyes when ever they saw a woman on the street in case they should lust. In consequence they often walked into brick walls and houses – hence the bruises and the bleeding! If a rabbi was seen speaking to a woman in public it was the end of his reputation.

In contrast to this Jesus treated women with the same equal respect which he showed to everyone else whom he met. Even though he was a Rabbi he went far beyond the accepted conventions of the time. On one occasion a woman who had been caught in adultery was brought to Jesus by some of the Pharisees and Teachers of the Law. In an effort to trap Jesus they reminded him that the law of Moses commanded that such women should be stoned to death. Jesus saw through their deceit and said if any one of them was without fault he should throw the first stone. On hearing this, they all slunk away in dismay. Jesus did not condemn the woman but told her to go and sin no more.

It is of enduring significance that after his resurrection the first people Jesus appeared to were women and most notably Mary Magdalene. She together with Joanna and Mary the mother of James were the first to publish the good news that he had risen from the dead. As soon as the Christian church was founded Jesus' valuing of women was reflected it its leadership. We find for example that there was a church in Laodicea led by Nympha and another at Cenchrea was served by Phoebe. Priscilla was a co-leader with her husband, Aquila, in one of the house churches in Rome. Mary, Junia, Tryphena, Tryphosa, Persis and Julia all appear to have had significant leadership roles in the congregations in the imperial city.[4] The first church in Philippi began in the house of Lydia, a seller of purple cloth. Two other leaders in that place were Euodia and Syntyche who had assisted in proclaiming the gospel.[5]

Throughout Christian history there have been many distinguished and godly women who have been Jesus' devoted followers and forwarded his kingdom work. Among those in earlier Christian times was Catherine of Alexandria. Tradition says that through her godly life and preaching she brought many to faith in her home city until the Roman Emperor Maxentius arrived on the scene. Unable to persuade her to deny her faith he instigated her cruel death having her bound to a chariot wheel. Few probably think of her when they set light to a Catherine wheel on bonfire night.

In more recent times Christian women have been prominent in the fight for equality and justice. Many have carried the gospel into distant lands and brought medical care and social improvement particularly in regards to temperance, child care and family life. In nineteenth century England Josephine Butler fought for the protection of prostitutes who, as the result of the Government's

---

[4] Romans 16:1-24
[5] Philippians 4:2-3

Contagious Diseases Act, were being brutally taken off the streets and examined to see if they carried venereal disease. In contrast, the men who used their services suffered no such treatment. Butler was also an ardent campaigner for equal rights and better education for women. In the same period in America, Harriet Tubman was a major figure in the campaign to abolish slavery and Frances Willard led two million members world-wide in a temperance movement. She also became a major campaigner for women's voting rights.

In 1903 with her mother Emmeline, Christabel Pankhurst founded *The Women's Social and political Union* and became the chief strategist of the Suffragettes. In 1918, the year British women achieved the vote, Christabel had a conversion experience which resulted in her becoming a powerful Christian preacher in Canada and America. That said, she never abandoned her feminism and continued to remind her audiences she was passionate for gender equality. The Suffragette, Emily Wilding Davies, was also a devout Christian who gave herself totally to the fight for equal rights and votes for women. She suffered in prison and even died for the cause when she took a risk running onto the race track in front of the King's horse at Epsom Downs in June 1913.

Coretta, the widow of Martin Luther King, carried forward the battle for racial equality after her husband's assassination. In more recent days the world has witnessed the powerful impact of Mother Teresa's care for the poor and dying on the streets of Calcutta. She summed up the feelings of many when she wrote: 'My poor ones in the world's slums are like the sufferings of Christ. In them God's son lives and dies, and through them God shows me his face'. Jackie Pullinger transformed lives of hundreds of drug addicts through prayer and her proclamation of Jesus' gospel in Hong Kong's old walled city of Kowloon. Heidi Baker's holistic evangelism has brought Christian hope and truck loads of food, shelter and provision to thousands in

Mozambique. Her story is beautifully told in her book *There will Always be Enough.*

It is clear that through the Christian centuries there have always been women of great distinction in every area of life who have found their inspiration and strength through following Jesus. Others include prominent social reformers such as Elizabeth Fry, Florence Nightingale, anti-slavery campaigners such as Lucretia Mott and Mary Anne McClintoch who founded the first American Anti-Slavery Society and national leaders including Prime Minister Teresa May and Queen Elizabeth II.

Jesus and politics

Jesus was political and he made political statements but recognising that politics is not reconciling he avoided attachment to any one particular party. Nowhere in his recorded teaching did he offer an answer to the Palestinian desire for deliverance from the ruling Roman authorities. He did not align himself with King Herod's party, the Herodians, on the one hand, nor on the other did he identify with the Zealots who wanted to overthrow the Roman army of occupation. In fact he made it clear that his followers should submit to lawful authority and pay their taxes to the Roman authorities. On the one occasion after he had fed five thousand men, and the women and children in addition, Jesus suddenly realized that the people were about to come and take him by force and make him their king so he fled into the nearby hills.[6] His disciples seem to have been slow to pick up on this particularly vital issue. When they met him after the resurrection at the time of Pentecost they asked him if he was about to restore the kingdom. His answer made it clear that he had no intention of restoring any kind of geographical

<hr>

[6] John 6:15

kingdom. His kingdom was not of this world.[7]

Perhaps part of Jesus' universal appeal is in this very fact that he is beyond the confines of any one political party. This is why in the USA there are dedicated Christians who are Republicans and Democrats and in England there are committed Christians in all the main political parties. It's also for the same reason that in some countries there are committed Christians who are Marxists. Just as Jesus transcends race, culture and class so he also transcends politics. Jesus' kingdom is one into which the people of every nation, race and culture can be a part. Nelson Mandela summed up the appeal of Jesus when he spoke at the Zionist Church's Easter Conference and said, 'The Good News is borne by our risen Messiah who chose not one race, who chose not one country, who chose not one language, who chose not one tribe, who chose all mankind'.

[7] Acts 1:6-8

CHAPTER 2
A Teaching for Everyone

One of the most obvious reasons for Jesus' universal appeal is the matchless quality of his straightforward teaching which is recognised by Christians, unbelievers, agnostics and adherents of other world faiths including Muslims. 'Nobody ever taught like this' was the conclusion of the crowds who heard Jesus speaking. Both Matthew and Mark record in their gospels that he instructed the people 'as one who had authority and not as one of the Scribes'. Jesus was a teacher who could say the most memorable things and in a vivid way that was not easily forgotten. It has been the conviction of people the world over that Jesus' teaching impresses itself on his hearers as being the truth. There is nothing in his teaching which has since been written off as erroneous. In fact there have been no ethical advances and no moral improvements since on the ways in which men and women should relate to one another. In response to the question, 'where did this man get his teaching from'? Jesus replied: 'My teaching is not mine, but his who sent me'.[8]

Jesus the Teacher

The New Testament uses various descriptions which indicate Jesus was a recognised teacher. Matthew uses the word 'Master' a term which means 'school teacher'. The disciples often addressed Jesus as 'teacher' as did the general public. In the New Testament

[8] John 6:16

Jesus is also called 'Rabbi' which could mean he was an official teacher in one of the synagogues. Jesus certainly used some of the rabbinical teaching methods but it is difficult to say much more than that. One thing is clear Jesus was a remarkable teacher and this is seen in both the method of his teaching as well as its content.

Jesus' teaching methods

Some of Jesus' teaching methods were not totally new and were used by the rabbis of his day. Such, for example, was his delight in hyperbolic statements and his frequent use of memory techniques. Scholars have translated parts of his *Sermon on the Mount* back from the Greek into the original Aramaic, the language Jesus and his disciples spoke. They found that it has a distinct poetic ring which would have made it easy to memorise. All the techniques the rabbis used were known to Jesus but he employed them with much greater effectiveness.

Drawing on the Old Testament

One of the obvious features of Jesus' teaching was his constant recourse to the Old Testament. He used the Old Testament Scriptures as the basis for most of what he taught. Furthermore he claimed to be the fulfillment of its prophecies about the coming of the Messiah. On one occasion Jesus said: 'Don't think I have come to do away with the law of Moses and the teachings of the prophets. I have not come to do away with them but to make them come true'. It is a fact that approximately one tenth of all the recorded words of Jesus in the gospels are direct quotations from the Old Testament. Jesus knew it well because he quoted from 24 of the 39 Old Testament books drawing particularly on Deuteronomy and the Psalms. The centre piece of his teaching is found in his best known Sermon on the Mount in which he showed the Ten Commandments should include people's thoughts and intentions as well as their outward actions.

Visual Content

Jesus was well aware that people are more likely to retain what is learnt through visual pictures rather than by words alone. This would have been particularly true of many of his hearers who were probably unable to read or write. Hence he often used every day things and events as his teaching aids. A sower on a hillside scattering seed caused him to liken people's responses to his teaching to different kinds of soil, some hard, stony and resistant but others well ploughed, fertile and able to produce a rich harvest. A meeting with the Pharisees clad in their long robes prompted him to warn people about pride and hypocrisy. A storm on the Sea of Galilee proved to be an opportunity for him to talk to the disciples about how to handle a crisis and trust him more fully.

Very close to drawing on every day events was Jesus' use of memorable homely illustrations. He communicated in 'street speak' always teaching in the language that ordinary people could readily understand. It was small wonder that 'the common people heard him gladly'. The down-to-earth character of what Jesus had to say comes out best in the stories he told about rebellious sons, parties where people didn't show up, sheep that went astray, garments that got eaten by moths, bad fruit trees and ill-prepared wedding guests.

Parables, proverbs and allegory

In his teaching methods Jesus used a variety of figures and

forms of speech the best known of which is the parable. The Greek word 'parable' means literally to place alongside. Something is set alongside an idea for the purpose of comparison or illustration. Jesus usually began with things that were very familiar to his hearers such as wayward sons, labourers working in a vineyard, lost coins, barren fig trees or yeast leavening bread. Then he related or compared them to some aspect of the kingdom of God. For this reason a parable has often been described as 'an earthly story with a heavenly meaning'. Part of Jesus' purpose in telling parables was simply so that people could discover truths for themselves. It often happened that those who listened went away remembering a great story and then suddenly some time later 'the penny dropped' and they got the spiritual punch line. Perhaps at first the parable of the Prodigal Son was remembered as a vivid story. Then later came the realisation that the father in the parable was a picture of the generous, forgiving and outgoing loving God.

Some of Jesus' parables were designed to stir individuals into action. The Good Samaritan and The Sheep and the Goats were stark reminders to care for those in need. Others were vivid pictures of the spiritual truths of God's kingdom. Among them were the Labourers in the Vineyard, the Great Supper Party and the Pearl of Great Price. The labourers who only managed to get work for the last hour of the day but got the same pay as those who had worked since the first hour was a powerful illustration of God's generosity. Those who come late to his kingdom would still enjoy the same full blessings as those of long-standing. The Great Supper made it obvious that being in the kingdom of God should be about joy, happiness, satisfaction and celebration.

As well as parables Jesus used proverbs and allegories such as the Vine and the Good Shepherd. Some of his proverbs have an enduring ring about them such as 'Sufficient unto the day is the evil thereof', 'the Sabbath was made for man, not man for the Sabbath' and 'You cannot serve God and money'. Jesus was also a master of satire and paradox. He called the hypocritical teachers of the law and the Pharisees of his day 'Blind guides! You strain a fly out of your drink', he said, 'but swallow a camel'! He warned a wealthy fellow countryman. 'It is much harder for a rich person to enter the kingdom of God than for a camel to go through the eye of a needle'! Among the most memorable of Jesus' paradoxical statements were, 'if any man would be first he shall be last of all and servant of all'[9] and again, 'He that loses his life', in other words spends it serving and helping others, 'will find it'.[10]

In his teaching Jesus was a master of argument, discussion and dialogue. When put on the spot by his religious opponents he often responded with a counter question. So when the Pharisees challenged him about healing people on the Sabbath he said to them, 'If any one of you had an ox that happened to fall into a pit on the Sabbath would you not pull him out on the Sabbath itself?[11]

The Kingdom of God

The heart of Jesus' teaching was the coming Kingdom of God. It was not, as some had hoped, a territorial or geographical kingdom but rather 'his spiritual rule in peoples' lives. It was not a far off Utopia or a distant future heaven it was right here and now. God's kingdom was found wherever He, the King, was ruling over people's lives. The kingdom of course required a particular standard of behaviour on the part of its citizens. Those who placed themselves under Jesus' rule were expected to adopt the lifestyle of the kingdom which he set out in his *Sermon on the Mount*.

[9] Matthew 20:16
[10] Matthew 10:13
[11] Luke 14:5

Behaviour in the kingdom

This sermon is a summary of the behaviour required by the citizens of his kingdom. In it he not only endorsed the teaching of the Ten Commandments but went on to show how they must impact our attitudes, thoughts and actions. The mere outward public keeping of the law isn't sufficient. What really matters are the inner motives, attitudes and feelings of the heart. It was why Jesus prefaced this teaching with the beatitudes or 'beautiful attitudes'[12] as they have sometimes been called. It is important that our interior life should be one of gentleness, mercy, purity of heart, peace, long-suffering and genuine sorrow over what is wrong in our lives together with prayer that prompts the living of the kingdom.

One of the key aspects we need to control is anger. We must not, Jesus stressed, allow it to fester because at root it is the spirit which leads to murder.[13] I have found, as I am sure you the reader have, that it is not a good idea to bottle up and suppress anger. It is a toxic emotion. It doesn't just raise our blood pressure; it can lead to seriously damaging effects on our physical well-being.

The same principle applies where adultery is concerned. Obviously it's wrong to commit adultery but to go on looking at another person with lustful desire is, Jesus argued, to commit adultery in the heart.[14] In Old Testament times men and women frequently took oaths to guarantee a particular course of action. As far as Jesus was concerned oaths should not be necessary as a simple 'yes' on the part of his followers should mean 'yes' and a 'no' mean 'no'.[15] His followers are to be people of their word who do exactly what they said they would do unless a sudden unforeseen situation made it impossible.

---

[12] Matthew 5:1-12
[13] Matthew 5:21-22
[14] Matthew 5:27-30
[15] Matthew 5:33-37

Jesus also instructed his followers to avoid aggression and to 'go the second mile' by which he meant that if a Roman soldier asked a person to carry his bags for the Empire's required one mile, his people were to be generous and make it two.[16] Additionally, if they were misused they were not to retaliate but rather turn the other cheek.[17] Indeed they were to love their enemies and pray for those who treated them spitefully.[18] They were to keep in mind that the enemy is not just the one who is out to take another person's life; he or she could be the one who maliciously destroys a good name or undermines a person's confidence.

Jesus, it should be noted, did not expect people to like their enemies or have affection for them but simply that they should love them, that is want to do the best for them. He urged his followers to avoid going to the law courts against one another and pleaded with them, if at all possible, that matters be settled amicably without having to go before a judge. By his well-known utterance 'render unto Caesar the things that are Caesar's but unto God the things that are God's'[19], Jesus left open the possibility that there might come a time when as a very last measure tyranny could be resisted with force. Jesus had a number of dealings with Roman military personnel but at no time did he condemn them for their profession.

At the very centre of Jesus' teaching is the fact that every human being is unique and uniquely precious in the sight of God. He made the point abundantly clear in a number of his parables most notably the lost sheep, the lost coin and the lost son. All three closely linked stories reveal a loving God caring and searching for broken and hurting men and women. On one occasion Jesus remarked that such was the divine love and concern for the whole of creation that not

---

[16] Matthew 5:41
[17] Matthew 5:38-39
[18] Matthew 5:43-44
[19] Mark 12:17

a single sparrow fell to the ground without his knowledge. How much more then, he went on to say, are men and women more valuable than many sparrows.

The Virtues

Significantly in all his teaching Jesus underlined the importance of the great virtues of faith, hope and above all of love. He constantly urged his followers to have a simple active trust in his guidance, protection and provision. He chided his disciples for their panic in a storm on the Sea of Galilee. He told those who were worried about food and clothing and what tomorrow might bring that they were people of 'little faith'. Jesus urged his followers to wear the badge of love. 'A new commandment I give you', he told his disciples, 'that you love one another even as I have loved you'.[20] By his many acts on behalf of the poor and needy Jesus taught the importance of being compassionate. In moments of unbelievable pain and agony as he suffered an unjust and brutal death on a cross Jesus underlined for ever the supreme importance of forgiveness as he uttered the words, 'Father forgive them they don't know what they are doing'.

Jesus' stressed the importance of purity and turning away from lust which he rightly saw could quickly lead to destructive relationships. He reasserted the commandment 'not to bear false witness' and underscored the importance of truth and being straight with people. It is, he so clearly stressed, 'the truth which sets us free'. He taught his followers to be worldly-wise people who would not readily have the wool pulled over their eyes. On one occasion he urged his disciples to be 'as wise as serpents and as harmless as doves'.[21] Jesus was for ever teaching his disciples patience and persistence. In his own personal life Jesus instructed by example the necessity of serving others, justice, courage, bravery, temperance and humility. Jesus rarely spoke of his own virtues but on at least one occasion he mentioned his own humility. 'Take my yoke upon you and learn from me', he told a Galilean crowd, 'for I am gentle and humble in heart, and you will find rest for your souls'.[22]

Marriage and divorce

Not only did Jesus set a high level on the value of the individual he was deeply concerned to uphold the sanctity and permanence of marriage. He laid down the basic foundational guide line that 'what God has joined together man must not separate'. His principle arose in response to the ease in which marriages at that time were being ended and often for the most trivial of reasons. Jewish Law was rooted in Deuteronomy 24:1 'If a man marries a woman who becomes displeasing to him because he finds something unclean about her, let him write her a bill of divorcement and send her out of the house'.

The question of what amounted to 'uncleanness' was hotly debated by the Jewish rabbis of the day. The strict school of Shammai said that uncleanness referred solely to un-chastity. In contrast the school of Hillel defined uncleanness in the very broadest of terms. They said a man could divorce his wife if for example she spoiled his dinner, went out in public with her head uncovered or if she merely talked with other men on the streets or was troublesome or quarrelsome. By the time of Jesus divorce was becoming ever more easy such that some young girls were even unwilling to get married because it had become so insecure. When Jesus said, 'I say to you every one who divorces his wife for any other cause than marital unfaithfulness'[23] he was making a serious attempt to stop these easy divorces he could see all around him.

---

[22] Matthew 11:29
[23] Matthew 19:9

He seriously wanted to reform the situation and strengthen the marital bond.

On the surface of it Jesus' standard on this matter seems overly demanding and he did say that not everyone could accept it. Indeed it is not difficult to understand the disciples' response that perhaps it was better not to marry at all! We should be clear that this was Jesus' ideal for his disciples. He fully recognised that people can only live out his teaching with the help of his divine presence and help in their lives. He was well aware that to sustain a marital relationship Christians need the love, sympathy, understanding, patience and forgiveness which only he could bring. He was also a realist and recognised that marriages, even where both husband and wife began as his committed followers, could change and degenerate. One or other or both partners might cease to practise their Christian faith and no longer uphold Jesus' ideal of one partner one life-time. No one can seriously believe that Jesus, the God of love and compassion, would require a husband or a wife to endure abusive treatment day in day-out. Indeed to allow such relationships to continue might well be dangerous to both partners as well as to any children in the home. Jesus' kingdom is clearly about new beginnings and it is hard to imagine that Jesus would not have wanted someone who had been badly and unjustly treated to have another opportunity to enjoy a loving and happy marriage.

Money and possessions

Jesus had nothing against money and wealth per se. It was only 'the love of money that is the root of all evil'. He was also clear that 'a man's life does not consist in the abundance of his possessions'. Jesus was categorical that no-one can serve two masters, God and money'. Jesus stressed the vital importance of living simply. He wisely counselled his disciples not to lay up treasures on earth where moth and rust corrupt and thieves break through and steal but to store up riches in heaven where there is no such decay or corruption. Jesus warned that we must never define or judge people by what they are worth in financial or wealth terms. He graphically illustrated the dangers of merely living for material things in his parable of the rich fool. The man in his story pulled down his barns and built larger ones in order to create room for more and more goods and crops and then on the very night he planned to sit back and enjoy it all, his life was snatched away.

At the very beginning of his ministry Jesus announced that he had come to bring 'good news to the poor'.[24] He warned of the dangers of ignoring their needs in his parable of the rich man and Lazarus. The wealthy tycoon gave no thought or concern for the needs of poor beggar Lazarus who lay covered in sores outside that main gate into his estate. But, in the after-life their situations were reversed and the rich man found himself in an even worse state than that which Lazarus had suffered in former times. It was then of course too late to do anything about it.

In his teaching Jesus constantly urged the vital importance of radical giving to those in need. In the *Sermon on the Mount* he instructed his followers to give and then they would find that it 'would be given back to them in good measure, shaken together and pressed down'. Here we are presented with the imagery of the corn market. In the first century a Judean woman would go to the merchant and pay for a certain amount of grain. It would often be tipped into her apron which she held out by the bottom corners. If the seller was generous it would be pressed down and was so full that it was spilling over. This delightful picture of generosity reminded me of a lovely couple who were part of a church

---

[24] Luke 4:18

I once led. The wife was a very generous and gifted American lady who often addressed women's conferences. She often spoke of the Lord as 'the much more father' who always returns more than we can give. Her husband was a very warm Scottish dentist with a slightly tight spot who once or twice told me that the English love the gospel because they can talk about it, the Welsh love it because they can sing it but the Scots love it because it's free!

In his searching parable of the sheep and the goats Jesus was clear that those who would be welcomed into the future kingdom would be those represented by the sheep who had provided food and drink for the hungry and thirsty, clothed the naked, welcomed the strangers and visited the prisoners. Those who failed to care represented by the goats would not find such a welcome.

Equality and justice

In all his teaching Jesus underlined the fact that every single individual was equally precious to God regardless of their sex, gender, creed, culture, colour, race or religion and must be treated with the same respect. As we have seen, Jesus constantly affirmed and treated women as his equals in a society which generally speaking denied them either recognition or respect. This was well-illustrated when Jesus took time out to talk with a woman of another faith at the well in the Samaritan village of Sychar and again when he healed the daughter of a Syrophoenician woman. In his best-known parable of *the Good Samaritan* Jesus was making the major point that people of another race and religious persuasion are to be valued as much as anyone else. Indeed in some instances they may even exceed our own religious leaders in their care and generosity. Jesus also emphasised the supreme importance of little children. He delighted in their company. He took them in his arms and blessed them and taught that they can indeed be members of his kingdom as much as any adult. By contrast his disciples had much to learn on this score. When they tried to send the children away from Jesus because they thought he was too busy he reprimanded them.

Jesus' stress on equality is clearly seen in the instructions that he gave for worship. At the Last Supper he specifically requested his followers to observe a simple act of eating bread and drinking red wine as the way of remembering and experiencing his covenant of love and forgiveness. The broken bread symbolised his body which he gave in sacrifice on the cross and the red wine depicted his innocent blood which cleanses the sins of the past. This was to be the New Passover and by so naming it Jesus made it clear that it should be similar in character to the Jewish Passover which it superseded. Adults and children and other members of the household sat as equals around the family table. It was to be in people's homes within the context of an evening meal preceded by the breaking and sharing of bread and ending after the supper had been eaten with the drinking of the wine. It was Jesus' intention that local leaders, merchants, fishermen, tax collectors, indeed men, women and children, rich and poor should come together as equal members of the family of God.

Jesus' teaching about Himself

The pinnacle of Jesus' teaching was what he taught about himself. His person and his message were uniquely inter-twined. What he taught and who he is could not be separated. Jesus didn't simply teach the truth, he claimed to be *the* truth. He didn't simply teach about a future resurrection, he said, 'I am the resurrection and the life'. Jesus didn't tell people the way to find God he declared himself to be God! On one occasion his disciple Philip asked Jesus to show him and his fellow disciples the Father. Jesus replied, 'If you have seen me you have seen the Father'.[25]

His own people the Jews had long believed and spoken of God as 'the Shepherd of Israel'. Most famously the 23rd Psalm says, 'The Lord is my Shepherd'. It also comes in Psalm 80 which begins with the words, 'Give ear, O Shepherd of Israel'. There are also references to Israel's God as being a shepherd in the writings of the Old Testament prophets Isaiah and Jeremiah. So when Jesus declared. 'I am the Good Shepherd',[26] he was making absolute claim to be nothing less than the God of Israel. It was for this reason that the Jewish religious leaders were so angry with him. They believed his claim to be God was blasphemous and so they sought to kill him. It was because Jesus was and is, nothing less than the human face of God, that he was able to forgive sins. Indeed the religious leaders 'got it'. 'For', they reasoned, 'who can forgive sins but God'.[27]

It was because Jesus knew himself to be wholly divine that he was freely able to forgive the sins of those who turned to him. This was why Jesus allowed people to worship him. When for example he restored the sight of a man who had been born blind, the man 'worshipped him'.[28] At a later point after he had risen from the dead Jesus appeared to Thomas and invited him to touch the scars on his wounded hands and side. In that moment his doubts were gone and he exclaimed, 'My Lord and my God'.[29] Some time later as Jesus was finally taken from the disciples into heaven they worshipped him'.[30] They clearly recognised him as 'the true God and eternal life'.[31]

---

[25] John 14:9
[26] John 10:11
[27] Mark 2:7
[28] John 9: 38
[29] John 20:28
[30] Luke 24:52
[31] I John 5.10

Jesus is, as Paul said, 'Our great God and Saviour'.[32] This is the bed-rock and foundation of everything else he taught. This is something beyond our human capacity to rationalise. It's akin to trying to put all the waters of a great ocean into a small drinking vessel. It doesn't fit! Jesus is the King of all Kings and the Lord of all Lords, the Mighty and Everlasting God. And yet he revealed himself as a human being and brought, and indeed brings, forgiveness through his death and resurrection.

A teaching for everyone

Jesus was by any standards a remarkable teacher. Not only did he teach high ethical standards of behaviour, he also modelled them in his own life. While a teacher's character probably doesn't significantly affect the teaching of geology, latin or mathematics that cannot be said of subjects that have a moral aspect to them. An adulterer clearly cannot teach purity with conviction nor can a grasping individual teach the importance and value of generosity. Moral truth cannot be adequately and convincingly taught solely in word it must be supported by example. No teacher has ever so completely embodied in their life the truth of what they taught save Jesus alone who claimed to be the truth.

Professor Norman Anderson, a specialist in Islamic theology, wrote: 'The teaching of Jesus stands on an Everest alone. No other teaching has had a comparable influence in countless lives and diverse cultures and ages'. What more fulfilling goal could there be than 'to love God with all your heart, mind, soul and strength and your neighbour as yourself'.[33]   No better summary   for human behaviour could be given than Jesus' 'Golden Rule' of do to others as

[32] Titus 2:13
[33] Luke 10:27

you would have them do to you'. Such is the enduring nature of Jesus' teaching that a very large proportion of the world's laws and culture are still rooted in its precepts. And where this is not overt it is probably the case that many of the western liberal social values of post-modernity are rooted in residual distillations of the Christian faith. Benjamin Franklin, one of the Founding Fathers of America, wrote in a letter to Ezra Stiles, 'As to Jesus of Nazareth, my opinion of whom you particularly desire, I think his system of morals and his religion, as he left it to us, the best the world ever saw, or is likely to see'. Lord Robert Boothby, a self-confessed atheist and one time private secretary to Winston Churchill, wrote, 'I believe the teachings of Jesus are the best that have yet been offered to mankind'. Perhaps it is apt to close this chapter by repeating its title and asserting that Jesus' straightforward words truly are a teaching for *everyone.*

CHAPTER 3
A Life Changing Experience

In 1517 Martin Luther, a German monk and teacher at the University of Wittenberg, put his trust in Christ for the very first time. He wrote that from that moment 'I felt myself to be reborn and to have gone through open doors into paradise. The whole of Scripture took on a new meaning...God became to me inexpressibly sweet in greater love'. On the evening of 24th May, 1738 John Wesley who was a discouraged Church of England clergyman attended an evening meeting at a little chapel at Aldersgate in the City of London. During the service he wrote that 'his heart was strangely warmed'. He felt that he trusted Christ alone and that 'he had taken away my sin, even mine and saved me from death'. Speaking on one occasion of his faith Cliff Richard said, 'If there is one thing I can recommend it has never been so good as from the time I became a Christian. It didn't change my career particularly but it did drastically change me and my attitude to my work, my attitude to other people and it's just made everything seem that much better'. Cliff went on to say that the thing 'that made my life really terrific, really valuable is the fact that Jesus entered it'. Christianity as it is meant to be is this kind of life transforming experience which comes through our relationship with Jesus.

This radical life change begins as we come to recognise who Jesus is and put our trust in him. He was born a human being and lived a human life on Earth for a little over thirty years. He had a fully human body. He ate and drank. He grew tired and weary. He experienced all the human emotions; love, joy, happiness, affection, loneliness, sadness, grief, physical abuse, persecution and death. He was brought up in an ordinary home by his parents Mary and Joseph along with his brothers and sisters. In all probability he worked alongside his father who was a carpenter. At some point in later life he became a synagogue teacher and gave himself entirely to reaching out in love and compassion to everyone he encountered teaching them about God's Kingdom. Wherever Jesus went he transformed people's lives.

Mary Magdalene lived on the dark side and was quite possibly a lady of the night. Hers was a world of moral and mental confusion but Jesus expelled her demons and she walked out of her past and became a compassionate and caring woman. Although Zacchaeus was a Jew, he worked as a tax collector for the Roman government. He was doubtless racked with guilt on account of overcharging and so defrauding his fellow countrymen. Jesus went to visit him in his home and persuaded him to do the right thing and repay those he had cheated. A lame man had lain beside the pool of Bethesda in Jerusalem for thirty-eight years. One day Jesus passed that way and told him to get up and take his mattress and walk. Bartimaeus was a blind beggar who sat by the roadside in Jericho. When Jesus came by he shouted out to him for help. Jesus restored his sight. Jesus declared that he had come to bring life in all its fullness. Wherever he went he brought a life changing experience. He fed the hungry, healed the sick, cast out the demons and preached good news.

When the risen Jesus was finally parted from his disciples he sent his unseen Holy Spirit presence into the lives of all who would step out in faith and trust him. Those who did so soon found their lives were transformed with a new attitude, a new mindset and a new strength. Jesus' small band of disciples who had all deserted him at his crucifixion suddenly found themselves filled with a new courage and a fresh boldness. They left their homeland and travelled out across the Roman Empire and by their preaching and living transformed its life and culture so that in the space of little more than two centuries it became a Christendom.

Through the succeeding centuries countless millions of people on every continent of the globe have followed Jesus and found the reality of this same life transforming presence. It's a transformation that brings with it a number of great benefits.

We're loved

The one thing which every single person in this world longs for is to love and be loved. The reason for this hard wiring is that we are made by a God who is love and in the image of a God who is love. It is small wonder that in the days when he was a young man, and before he became a Christian, St Augustine wrote, 'The single desire that dominated my search for delight was simply to love and be loved'. The C20th philosopher, Bertrand Russell, wrote on the 25th July, 1956, 'I have sought love, first, because it brings ecstasy so great that I would have sacrificed all the rest of my life for a few hours of this joy...next because it relieves loneliness. Finally, because it is a prefiguring of heaven'.

The heart and core of the Christian faith is that we're loved by God unconditionally, not for anything we've done or deserved but simply for who we are. Every single person in the entire world is different. We all have a unique hand print, voice print, iris print and DNA. Unsurprisingly therefore each one of us is individually loved by God. He made us and he loves us as a parent loves a child.

As St Augustine once said, 'God loves us as if there is only one of us to love'. It has been said that nothing can make God love us more and nothing can make him love us less.

One of the most quoted verses in the entire Bible is in John's Gospel chapter 3 verse 16 that says God so loved this world that he came and lived in it in the person of Jesus. God's love is more than mere sentiment, it's a fact of history. Jesus demonstrated this love by giving and spending himself in serving others. Finally he made the ultimate sacrifice of love by dying the death our sins deserve. As he once said, 'Greater love has no man than this that he lay down his life for his friends'.[34]

Jesus' clear promise was 'As the father has loved me, so have I loved you. Now remain in my love'.[35] Knowing that we are fully loved by our maker enables us to love ourselves, to feel good about ourselves and to be comfortable in our own skin. It also gives us the confidence to build relationships with others. In short, it enables us to love our neighbours for, as Jesus reminded us, we can't love our neighbours if we have no love for ourselves. Bear Grylls, adventurer and chief Scout, once said, 'I always get asked difficult religious questions wherever I go and do you know what I sometimes say is, I don't know but I know I am loved'.

We're forgiven

Because God loves he also forgives. Forgiveness is another fundamental human need which lies at the heart of Jesus' teaching. We all carry emotional baggage which includes anxiety, sorrow, worry, depression, sadness and a host of other scars and pains resulting from mistakes we have made, abuse we have suffered or hurtful things we

---

[34] John 15:13
[35] John 15:9

have done. We are capable of great acts of love and kindness but we can also cause great hurt to others, even those who are the nearest and dearest to us. In consequence we find ourselves with varying amounts of guilt. Much of it plays out in our conscious minds. Some of it is subconscious and lies below the surface of our general thinking but has a habit of rising up to the surface in moments of stress or conflict. We also have deep within ourselves unconscious guilt resulting from experiences such as trauma, abuse, rejection and other deeply hurtful things from way back. The pain from these issues can lie buried deep in our unconscious minds. Unbeknown to us they may even be having a dysfunctional effect on our daily living.

The truth of the matter is that we all carry some form of guilt. And we need to get rid of it both for the sake of our emotional well-being and general health. In his autobiographical novel *The Road to Wigan Pier* George Orwell who was not a Christian, reflected on the bitterness and remorse he experienced from his brutal work with the colonial police in India. After recalling the faces of numerous prisoners in the dock, of men waiting in condemned cells, of subordinates he had bullied and servants and coolies he had hit', he wrote, 'I was conscious of an immense weight of guilt I had to expiate'.

We can't rid ourselves of this guilt. Nor can we say to someone 'Your sins are forgiven'. We are simply just another imperfect fellow human being. One of the Old Testament Psalm writers expressed it powerfully writing, 'No man can redeem the life of another or give God a ransom for him'. The good news of the Christian gospel is that the God of the universe has done just that. He stepped into this world becoming a man in the person of Jesus. Living an exemplary and perfect life he reached out in love and compassion to everyone who is willing to turn away from what is evil and wrong, and trust him and say, 'Your sins are forgiven'![36]

Jesus' gift of forgiveness came through his supreme act of love in dying on a cross outside the city of Jerusalem. There he died the death our sin, selfishness and hurtful acts deserve. As he, the God of Creation, hung suffering with excruciating pain, the gospel writers record that 'darkness fell over the place of crucifixion for three hours'.[37] At the end of that time Jesus cried out in triumphant agony, 'It is finished'! He had conquered human sin and broken its power and guilt. Somehow in a way we will never fully understand Jesus' perfect offering of himself overcame and absorbed all the unrighteousness and the hurt perpetrated by the human race. St Paul expressed it this way, 'Jesus who knew no sin was made sin for us'.[38] The apostle Peter also wrote, 'Jesus himself bore our sins in his body on the cross'.[39]

On the occasion of her Diamond Jubilee in 1889 Queen Victoria issued a free pardon to all those who had deserted from her armed forces during the course of her reign. It was advertised with a response form in most of the major newspapers. Those who wanted to receive clemency were requested to fill in their details and send it to the specified address. When they had completed their personal application they then received their official pardon. In a similar way God in the person of Jesus offers a full and free pardon to everyone who asks to receive it. All that is required is that we apply to him personally in the same way as we would speak to anyone who we respect and say from the very depth of our heart, 'Lord Jesus, God and Saviour' I turn away from all that is wrong in my life and I receive your personal pardon and forgiveness.

---

[36] Mark 2:5 & 9
[37] Matthew 27:45 and Luke 23:44
[38] 2 Corinthians 5:21
[39] 1 Peter 2:21

Once we have taken that step and truly turned away in sorrow from all that has been wrong in our past we are truly absolved and our guilt is cleansed away. The presence of Jesus' Holy Spirit then enters into our inner beings and makes his forgiveness a reality in our experience. That said, we will still need to keep short accounts with him. This means that on every future occasion when we mess up or cause hurt we need to ask for his forgiveness again and for the help to keep us walking in his way. The apostle John wrote that 'if we continue to live in the light of Jesus' presence' and 'keep on confessing our sins to him when they happen we will be cleansed and purified from all unrighteousness'.[40] *The Letter to the Hebrews* says, 'the blood of Christ through the eternal Spirit will cleanse our consciences'.[41]

Down through the ages hundreds of thousands of men and women have found the reality of this same forgiveness and freedom. John Bunyan in his allegory, *The Pilgrim's Progress*, likened it to a great burden being rolled away. When Christian, the central character in the story, 'came to a place where there stood a Cross the burden that he carried was loosed from his shoulders and fell from his back'. Charles Wesley, the great Methodist leader and brother of John, likened this forgiveness in one of his hymns to being loosed from the shackles of a prison, 'My chains fell off, My heart was free, I rose went forth and followed Thee'.

Receiving and knowing the Jesus' forgiveness is the beginning of this truly life-transforming experience. It marks the start of a whole new chapter in our lives. As Paul wrote, 'If any man is in Christ he is a new creation'.[42]

---

[40] 1 John 1:7-9
[41] Hebrews 9:14
[42] 2 Corinthians 5:17

A New Birth.

From the moment anyone receives Jesus' forgiveness his Spirit is present in them. Paul reminded the followers of Jesus 'that after they had believed they were marked with a seal, the promised Holy Spirit'.[43] He also wrote similarly to the Corinthian church that Christ has 'set his seal of ownership on us, and put his spirit in us'.[44] This is a metaphor we readily understand. If the King or Queen approves or accepts a product it is endorsed by their seal, stamped with the royal coat of arms. When we have received the gracious forgiveness of Jesus our King and been accepted by him he seals us with his stamp of approval which is his Spirit. For some this sealing can be a feeling of intense joy and overwhelming love. For others it may simply be a deep awareness of peace and well-being. For those who have been hatefully treated, received great hurt or been in prison, the experience of conversion can be an overwhelming sense of release and forgiveness. Much probably depends on our individual character and the circumstances surrounding the moment of our commitment to Christ. Either way once we have been sealed by the Spirit we have an inner conscious awareness that we belong to Jesus and that he has his hand on our life.

The experience of the New Birth sometimes puzzles nominal church-goers and even Christian leaders. On one occasion Jesus met with Nicodemus a religious leader in Jerusalem. He had been captivated by the miraculous signs Jesus was doing. Not wanting to lose the respect of his fellow Jewish leaders he visited Jesus after dark when he was less likely to be seen by anyone important. He was a respected theologian but Jesus had to tell him straight that no-one can see the kingdom of God unless he is born again'.[45] Nicodemus was

---

[43] Ephesians 1:13
[44] 2 Corinthians 1:21
[45] John 3:3

bemused by the talk of a 'new birth' and said, 'How can a man be born again when he is old? Surely he cannot enter a second time into his mother's womb and be born'? Jesus then told him not to confuse 'the new birth' with 'physical birth' because the new birth is a spiritual birth. New birth is his divine Spirit in us assuring us that we're forgiven and implanting in us the desire, strength and resolve to live our lives Jesus' way. To be 'born again' is to be changed inwardly by Jesus' Spirit in us creating a whole new way of life. This new birth experience leads to new character.

A New Character

In a number of places the New Testament speaks of believers as people who are 'in Christ'. Paul reminded those in Rome that 'there is no condemnation for those who are 'in Christ'.[46] He prayed for the Christians in Ephesus that 'Christ would dwell 'in their hearts'.[47] To the congregations in Galatia he wrote of 'Christ living in me'[48] and he reminded the church in Corinth that 'we have the mind of Christ'.

From these and other New Testament verses it is clear that Christians are people who have the presence of Christ living within them. No wonder the Apostle Paul wrote of 'the mystery which is Christ in you' and of 'Christ who is our life'.[49] If the presence of Jesus is in a person's mind and feelings we would expect their attitudes and living to begin to reflect Christ-like qualities. And this is in fact the central aspect of the life transforming experience which is birthed in the lives of those who receive Jesus' forgiveness and commit their lives to following him. We see something of how this

---

[46] Romans 8:1
[47] Ephesians 3:17
[48] Galatians 2:20
[49] Colossians 3:4

worked out in the quaintly written autobiography of Billy Bray an eighteenth century Cornish mine worker. Entitled *The King's Son* Bray describes how he fell into bad habits as a young man and was frequently drunk and in debt. But in November 1823 his life dramatically changed after he had first read John Bunyan's *Visions of Heaven* and then his *Visions of Hell*. It caused him to go upstairs to the bedroom where he cried out to the Lord to save him. He recorded that 'in an instant he made me so happy that I cannot express what I felt. I shouted for joy'. He remembered that 'Everything looked new to me, the people, the fields, the cattle, the trees. I was like a man in a new world'.

Not everyone will experience the new birth in quite such as dramatic way as Billy Bray but all who decide to follow Jesus will at the very least notice a gradual transformation in their thinking, values and behaviour. This doesn't mean we can sit back and expect to become saints over-night because we are human beings with minds and wills of our own. We have to make a constant conscious effort to say and to do the right things as Jesus' spirit prompts us. The great encouragement is that his Spirit strengthens us and gives us the will to live the new life. Sadly of course it often happens that the followers of Jesus drift or walk away from his ways and his promptings and he is dishonoured.

Jesus was clear that with his help we who are his followers are called to live out the new birth that has been implanted in us by his Spirit. We are to let his light shine through our good works. Jesus' presence in a believer will positively impact every aspect of their life and being.

There are however nine particular qualities or fruit of the Holy Spirit which form the essence of the life-changing experience which the New Birth of Jesus' presence brings into our lives. They are virtues which we have to work to grow and develop but always with the help of his Holy Spirit. They are love, joy, peace, patience, kindness, goodness, faithfulness, gentleness, and self-control. The remainder of this chapter considers each of these in turn.

We will grow in Love

If we are committed followers of Jesus we will experience the steady flow of his love into our lives.[50] This in turn enables us to love others with that same love. Jesus' divine love differs from family love, affection and eroticism. It's primarily something we do rather than feel. It's a sacrificial love for which the Greeks had a separate word which is agape. The agape love of Jesus is an active, outgoing, caring, kind and compassionate love. It's the quality Jesus demonstrated to the full in his time on Earth. In fact Jesus said we can and we must try to love even our enemies. When Jesus commanded his followers to love one another it was always the kind of outgoing self-giving love. John recounts that the risen Jesus rebuked the early Church in the city of Ephesus because 'they had lost their first love for him'. Their enthusiasm for him had withered away. He had to exhort them to do again the things they had done in the beginning.

In his *Letter to the Corinthians* Paul reminds us of some of the characteristics of Christian love, 'It is not envious, does not boast, is not self-seeking, is not rude and it's always truthful, always protects and always perseveres'.[51] Indeed he ends by stating that it is the supreme virtue because love is the very nature of God.

Jesus was clear that if we obey and live out his commands his love will continue to flow through us to others. As Mother Teresa said, 'Small acts of service done with great love change the world'. And as the New Testament says, 'Love covers a multitude of sins'.

---

[50] Romans 5:5
[51] 1 Corinthians 13:4-7

So if someone treats us unkindly or speaks ill of us we pray for them. We bless them in some way with an act of love.

We have a new Joy

The Greek word for joy which Jesus promised is almost the same as the word for grace. Joy is not quite the same as happiness because happiness is often dependent on outward situations. As someone once said, 'Happiness is about what happens to you'. Such is not the case with joy. In his letter to some of his fellow Christians who were suffering for their faith, James wrote what seems to be almost a contradiction in terms. 'Consider it pure joy my brothers', he urged, 'whenever you face trials of many kinds'.[52] How ever hard our Christian journey we can still experience joy. In fact Jesus said that even when people slander or mistreat us we can still have joy.[53] He promised his followers 'my joy will be in you that your joy may be complete'.[54] We have joy within us because Jesus' presence in us is joy. Nevertheless we still have to make the effort to live out that joy and be joyful. That's why the Apostle Paul wrote in his *Letter to the Philippians*, 'Rejoice in the Lord always and I will say it again, Rejoice'.[55] In the Greek it's actually a command to be joyful. We can choose to be Mr Grumpy or Mr Miserable for a day if we want, but it's not part of the transformed life that we have been chosen for. We must make the effort to be positive and glad. William Barclay, a Professor from the University of Glasgow, was right when he wrote, 'A gloomy Christian is a contradiction in terms, and nothing in all religious history has done Christianity more harm than its connection with black clothes and long faces'.

---

[52] James 1:2-4
[53] Matthew 5:11-12
[54] John 15:11
[55] Philippians 4:4

We will know a new kind of peace

In fact the Bible calls the peace which Jesus gives 'a peace that passes all understanding'.[56] That means it's an experience but we can't rationalise or account for it. It's more than the absence of hostility or any kind of distressing situation. Peace is more than an inner calm or tranquillity. The Hebrew word 'shalom' which is found in many places in the Old Testament and is the equivalent Greek word 'irene' both mean wellness, harmony and fullness of life. The word 'peace' occurs several hundred times in the Bible and many of the New Testament letters begin or end with a greeting of peace. As was the case with joy, peace is not dependent on calm or tranquil circumstances. It's an inside job. Outwardly a situation could be demanding but we can still know peace within.

The prophet Isaiah foretold that Jesus would come as 'the Prince of Peace'. So it proved. There were many occasions when he brought peace. There was an occasion when the disciples were panicking because their boat appeared to be sinking in a storm. Jesus stood up and rebuked the wind and the rain and there was a great calm. After he had healed a woman who had suffered a blood flow for many years he said to her, 'Go in peace your faith has made you well'. On the evening of the day when he rose from the dead Jesus appeared to his disciples in a room where they were hiding for fear of the Jews and said, 'Peace be with you and he showed them his hands and his feet'. St Paul wrote that 'Christ Himself is our peace',[57] and John recorded Jesus' appearing to his disciples after rising from the tomb and saying, 'Peace be with you'.

From the very moment we first put our trust in Jesus our inner conscious being begins to fill with a new and deep-seated peace. Paul wrote that once we have trusted the Lord for forgiveness of all

---

the past wrong in our lives 'we have peace with God'.[58] Peace flows into our lives because the presence of Jesus, the Prince of Peace, is living in us. But we for our part have to consciously live out that peace by our words and actions. We must pray as St Francis did, 'Make me an instrument of your peace' and then follow Jesus' call to go out and be 'peacemakers'.[59]

We will grow in patience

We live in an impatient world which expects instant solutions and rapid results. Like the white rabbit in *Alice in Wonderland* we are too often looking at our watches and running somewhere in a hurry. But the transforming presence of Jesus in us will gradually enable us to become more patient. The Greek word for patience also carries this same idea of self-restraint or 'self-control'. The English word patience is derived from the Latin word 'patio' meaning to suffer.

Patients are people who suffer in pain or sickness. Patience includes an element of suffering. Patience is not just waiting; it's what we do while we are waiting. In order to maintain good relationships we sometimes have to be patient and avoid retaliating when somebody misrepresents us or speaks harshly to us. Exercising such self-restraint often causes us emotional pain but we know that patience is the only way to proceed. Waiting for the right opportunity to come, holding on to someone's promise, tolerating a difficult neighbour or family member all require patience.

Jesus' life was marked by patience. His disciples could be very frustrating at times. Sometimes he even called them dullards. They were slow learners who often missed the point. Instead of showing love and compassion to the marginalised and needy they wanted to know what they were going to get out of following him.

---

[58] Romans 5:1
[59] Matthew 5:9

Jesus displayed supreme patience at the time of his illegal trial and death. When he was whipped, beaten and forced to wear a crown of thorns he did not retaliate. Despite having false accusations and trumped up charges made against him he remained graciously silent.

Jesus' presence living in us will gradually increase our ability to be patient. With his help we will find ourselves able to be more tolerant with people especially those who interrupt us when we're busy, criticise us with harsh words or let us down. The Lord will help us to be patient with the unsolved issues we carry within ourselves and questions that cannot be readily or easily answered.

We will grow in kindness

Another aspect of the transforming presence of Jesus in our lives is that we will find ourselves growing in kindness. In Jesus' parable of the Good Samaritan who came to the aid of the man who fell among the thieves on the road from Jerusalem to Jericho we have a wonderful picture of kindness. The Samaritans and the Jews were sworn enemies and yet the good man who came to the rescue was a Samaritan. He bound up the man's wounds, took him to an Inn and paid for his care. Jesus ended the parable with the plea to all his followers to go and do likewise.

Whereas in time past we might well have passed by someone we could easily have stopped to help we now find ourselves prompted to take action. Kindness is closely related to compassion. Kindness is endeavouring to help someone who is in need or in a difficult situation. Compassion is the ability to feel for them in their time of need. Many people instinctively think of real Christians as people who are kind and compassionate such as Florence Nightingale whose Christian faith eventually led her to go out in 1854 to nurse the many British soldiers who had been badly injured in the Crimean war. Charles Dickens famous novel *A Christmas Carol* is the story of how the miserly Scrooge became kind and caring. Dickens begins his last published book *The Life of Our Lord* with these words.

> My dear children, I am very anxious that you should know something about the history of Jesus Christ. For everybody ought to know about Him. No one ever lived, who was so good, so kind, so gentle, and so sorry for all people who did wrong, or were in any way ill or miserable, as He was.

Kindness issues in practical compassionate care. We see it for example in Brian Souter's compassionate practical action. An active Christian and the owner of Stage Coach he gives generous support to many social and community needs. This is spot on because Jesus said that the light of his presence is seen by his followers doing acts of kindness. These might be small everyday acts of kindness; giving a coffee to a rough sleeper, helping a stranger push a broken down car to the side of a road, visiting a lonely neighbour and a host of other similar gestures. The moral of Aesop's fable 'The Lion and the Mouse' is that 'no act of kindness, no matter how small, is ever wasted'. The nineteenth century American philosopher Ralph Waldo Emerson once wisely wrote, 'You cannot do a kindness too soon, for you never know how soon it will be too late'. We need to take note of Paul's reminder of the 'kindness of God our Saviour' who 'created us to do good works'.[60]

Our lives will be marked by Goodness

Very closely related to kindness is the virtue of goodness. The Greek word for 'good' is kalos which describes a thing that is good in its very nature. Jesus, our God and Saviour, cannot be other than good

---

[60] Ephesians 2:10

because that is his very nature. In Jesus we see that God is good all the time. Because all human beings are created in the image of God every single person has some innate sense of what goodness is. Some have it in strong measure and we recognise them as good men or good women. Barnabas, an early apostle and travelling companion of Paul is described as 'a good man'. Being a good person is not about being a 'goodie-goodie'. It's about standing strong for what is right and just in the face of opposition. Maximilian Kolbe, a Roman Catholic Franciscan Friar serving in German occupied Poland, was thrown into prison because of his outspoken stance against the Third Reich. Eventually he was released but instead of adopting a low profile he continued to publish anti-Nazi material. This time he was sent to Auschwitz. There his goodness was supremely visible. When a minor public disturbance took place several men were rounded up and chosen to be executed. Kolbe heard a man crying out, 'But my wife and my children'. Kolbe who was unmarried immediately volunteered to die in his place. In recognition of his goodness he was canonised as a saint in 1982.

Goodness is both about our nature or character as well as our actions. As well as being totally good by nature Jesus revealed his goodness in his guidance, provision, forgiveness and his care for others. Goodness is also seen in terms of excellence. In the everyday we speak of people who do their work well and conscientiously as good teachers, good administrators, good shop managers or whatever they happen to be.

Good people are like an orange no matter how hard it is squeezed only sweetness comes out. Goodness is most obvious when a person is suffering, persecuted or abused because no bitterness comes out of them. Such is the goodness we see in Jesus.

While brutal Roman soldiers hammered nails through his hands and feet his only response was, 'Father forgive them'. Jesus' Spirit, which is total goodness, has been planted in us in the moment we committed our lives to him and begins to grow in the way that a small seed gradually develops into a plant.

Faithfulness

The Greek word which the New Testament uses for faith in Jesus is more than mere intellectual assent. It means active trust. Martin Luther distinguished what he called 'historic faith' from what he termed 'true faith'. 'Historic faith' gives intellectual assent to the facts about Jesus while true faith commits itself to the facts. True faith in Jesus is to entrust our lives to him. It is to trust that he has forgiven our sins and that our life and destiny are in his hands. True faith is to rely on the fact that Jesus is there beside us and will always be there for us throughout life's journey and beyond.

As well as being an active daily trust, faith also has to do with character. A faithful person is reliable, dependable and trustworthy by nature. We sometimes describe such people as 'rock-solid' or just 'rocks' or even 'a brick'! A faithful friend doesn't give up on us. A faithful servant doesn't let his or her employer down. Just as the TV advert says, 'It does what it says on the tin'; faithful people are the same. What they say they will do they will do. They are as good as their word.

Jesus is 'faithful over the household of God'. He is the one 'who is faithful and true'. During the first three centuries of the Christian era literally thousands of believers were severely persecuted by the pagan officials of the Roman Empire. Many died for their faith rather than deny Jesus and declare that 'Caesar is Lord'. Today Jesus' presence in us strengthens us to be faithful in standing for what we know to be right and true. It enables us to be faithful in our relationships, marriage, family life and in our dealings with money.

Gentleness

Gentleness is a quality which is often neglected and underrated. This is due to the fact that it is frequently regarded as effeminate or a mark of weakness. The reality however is quite the reverse. Gentleness is controlled strength. Indeed some people have for this very reason been called 'gentle giants'. Yes, it is possible to be both gentle and a giant at the same time. Jesus is depicted both as like a Lion meaning strength and a lamb symbolising gentleness. Moses was a respected leader who led the people of Israel out of slavery in Egypt. Yet we're told that 'he was very meek, more than all men that were on the face of the earth'.[61] Michelangelo's statue of Moses in the Church of St Peter-in-Chains in Rome depicts him as impressively powerful and yet before God and in his dealings with God's people he was gentle.

The Greek word for gentleness is also used of animals which have been brought under control. After a cart horse has been broken in, it is just as powerful as before but its controlled strength enables it to be put to effective and good use. People who are gentle are sensitive and considerate. They don't barge in on the act and start to tell people what's what. Rather, they tread softly and ease themselves into the situation. They are respectful of people and situations and try always to get a sense of what is happening. St Francis of Assisi has been called 'the gentle revolutionary'. Gentlemen are gentle! They are considerate, polite and aware of other people's needs. Gentle people are not quick to stand on their own rights. They are not in the business of trying to convince

---

[61] Numbers 12:2

everyone that they know the answers and are always right. They recognise the truth that overwhelming power can win a battle but still lose a war. Jesus' life was marked by constant gentleness especially with women, children, the lepers and the marginalised. If we keep in constant communication with him by praying and consciously remembering he is with us we will find ourselves becoming more gentle in nature and in our dealings with others.

We will develop greater self-control

The western world in particular is a growingly addictive one. Too many of us are enslaved to our phones, Face Book, the internet and Twitter. Others are hooked on alcohol, drugs, entertainment and retail therapy. One thing is patently clear, we need self-control. We have to admit that at times our lives are like being on a hamster wheel. Sometimes they literally spin ever faster and we just can't get off. Not all of our activities and business concerns are necessarily bad in themselves but too much of many of them is manifestly not good for us. Effective lives need balance and moderation. Self-control is therefore a vital ingredient which everyone needs to practice.

The most obvious aspects of our lives which need self-control are our tempers and our eating and drinking. Paul reminds us that a Christian's body is the temple of the Holy Spirit. His use of the word 'temple' is significant because a temple is a sacred building which needs to be treated with reverence and respect. Jesus' presence in us will inevitably prompt us to take better control of any areas of our lives where we are being driven to excess be that our behaviour, our work, leisure or calorie intake. It often happens that we have an Achilles' heel or one major weak spot where we are particularly vulnerable. It may be anger, sex, pornography, drink, spending or a host of other things. Whatever the issue happens to be this is where we need to pray for help and then resolve and determine that we are going to take control of the situation.

Jesus taught that self-control requires strong disciplinary measures. He said, 'If your eye offends you cut it out'. He didn't mean that literally. His point was if we find ourselves compulsively looking at bad material on the internet, turn it off or lock it out. Equally he said, 'if your hand offends you cut it off'. He simply meant that if we find our hands are about to get involved in some kind of dishonest practice walk away; don't go there! To be self-controlled also of course means to take control of our tongue, to think before we speak and to ensure we always speak what is pure, just, true, loving and encouraging. Winston Churchill once said, 'I have had to eat my words on many occasions and a very healthy diet it has proved to be'. To be self- controlled requires us to avoid anything that is extreme, excessive, fanatical, unbalanced or over-the-top. The New Testament exhorts us to let our moderation be known to everyone.

Exercising this kind of self-control demands rigorous effort. It is something we see in the lives of great athletes. A runner needs to keep running every day in order to keep fit and be in top condition. He or she needs to be disciplined in their eating and sleeping habits. Laziness would be fatal. In a way similar to the athlete Paul urged Timothy to tell people 'to train themselves to be godly'.[62] Olympic runners practice self-discipline so that they can win the race, achieve gold and bring honour to their nation. Like the athlete we too need the discipline of self-control so that we can win the crown of life and bring honour to Jesus our Lord.

---

[62] I Timothy 4:7

Growing in these life-changing qualities.

These nine life-changing qualities that we have been considering in this chapter the New Testament calls 'fruit of the Spirit'.[63] As we have seen they are the fruit of the seeds of which are sown in us from the moment we first put our trust in Jesus our God and Saviour. All these qualities exist in perfection in him. As we begin and continue to live in him and seek his help and presence in our lives they begin to grow in us. We can also help to nurture them further by praying, self-discipline, reading the Gospels, worshipping and meeting with other Christians.

[63] Galatians 5: 22

CHAPTER 4
An Exemplary Leader To Follow

M any books have been written on leadership and many more will follow. Among those who are considered in books and on web sites to be great leaders are the Emperor Augustus, Catherine of Alexandria, Abbess Hilda, Martin Luther, George Washington, Horatio Nelson, Abraham Lincoln, Florence Nightingale, Catherine Booth, Winston Churchill, Margaret Thatcher, and Nelson Mandela. Strangely perhaps most seem to have overlooked the leadership of Jesus. This is surprising, because far more people living on the face of this planet have followed and do follow Jesus than any other person. So it therefore makes more than good sense to examine why Jesus is such a universal, effective and significant leader.

Visionary focused leadership

The one vital quality every leader must have is a clear vision which they can impart to their followers in such a way that they can understand it and run with it. Every effective leader the world has ever seen has this ability to present such an agenda and then inspire others to embrace it.

Jesus came to bring about a totally new kind of kingdom on planet Earth. His kingdom was not a political one or a geographical territory. He came to call men and women to live their lives in a totally new way relating to each other with an outgoing unselfish and caring love. At the start of his ministry Jesus gave a sermon in the synagogue at Capernaum in which he set out his supremely important kingdom values of freedom, forgiveness, healing and wholeness. He constantly focused his disciples on this vision until with the passing of time it became their vision.

Servant leadership

Jesus modelled a new kind of leadership. He entered this world as the Lord of the universe. Yet he was never in any way over-bearing or demanding. He came to establish a unique model of leadership – servant leadership. Jesus was born King of the Jews but in reality he was, and is, far more than that. He is 'the King Eternal'[64], the King of Kings[65] and ruler of the Universe. Yet, unlike the world's rulers, he didn't stand on his status, manipulate, use or seek to dominate others with a show of power. He came into the world as a 'servant king'. Jesus' leadership still stands in stark contrast to that of the great political leaders in world history. In fact Jesus uttered stern warnings that his followers were not to be like the rulers of the nations of the world and their high officials 'who Lord it over' the people. 'Instead', he said, 'whoever wants to be the greatest among you must be your servant, and whoever wants to be first must be the servant of all'. Jesus then asserted that 'he had not come to be served but to serve'.[66]

Jesus' way was to inspire others by serving them without any strings attached. This was the reason why at the close of his ministry at the Last Supper he picked up a towel and a bowl of water and took on the servant's task by washing his disciples' feet. He then said to them,

[64] 1 Timothy 1:17
[65] Revelation 17:14
[66] Mark 10:42-44

'If I your Lord and Master have washed your feet, you also ought to wash one another's feet'.[67] In other words, we're to follow his exemplary pattern of servant-hood.

Many of those who the world takes to be great leaders don't stand out as having a servant nature. Most are dominant authoritarian figures of the Trump and Putin variety. Their top-down, managerial styles of leadership don't engage with people at a personal level and fail to produce a heart-felt loyalty. Inevitably in companies, and indeed in churches, this kind of dominant leadership tends to produce people whose loyalty and commitment lasts only for a relatively short period. As has often been said, 'Power tends to corrupt and absolute power tends to corrupt absolutely'.

Jesus therefore taught his disciples that leaders are to become servants. They are not to be dictatorial or to set out to dominate and control others. Servants are attentive listeners. They heed the voices of the people they serve. Jesus modelled servant leadership by working with and for others. Jesus didn't control or do everything; he shared leadership with his disciples. It is significant that the leaders Jesus chose to work with him eventually followed his model of servant leadership. We find his early co-workers Peter, Paul, James, Jude and John all refer to themselves as 'servants of Christ'. Diotrephes an early Christian leader mentioned by John on the other hand was roundly rebuked for always seeking the pre-eminent place in the church's leadership.[68]

A limited glimpse of what servant-hood might mean in more recent times was seen in the life of William Kelvin, a Scottish engineer, and an expert in electricity. When the first electric cable was being laid in Glasgow he worked in a trench wearing dungarees alongside the labourers. An interested young student who happened

---

[67] John 13:14
[68] 3 John 9

to pass by at the time looked down at him in a condescending manner and remarked, 'What do you know about electricity'? The great authority looked up at him and said, 'Not very much I'm afraid'. No-one could tell in that moment that Kelvin was the greatest authority on electricity at that time. His status was hidden as he quietly worked alongside the men in a humble servant manner.

Non-hierarchical shared leadership

Anyone who is a servant clearly does not sit at the top of a hierarchy. Servants are not bosses. They don't operate from a distance and issue instructions from an executive suite. They serve. When Jesus set out the strategy for his kingdom he didn't create a hierarchy with himself as the front man. Rather, he established what was, in effect a flat team of co-workers. He worked with them not over them. Non-hierarchical leadership is shared leadership. He told his disciples, 'I have called you friends, for everything that I have learned from my Father I have made known to you'.[69]   Jesus recognised that in order for a vision to be carried forward in an effective way it needs to be shared. Then your followers become co-workers. In the end your vision becomes their vision.

Leaders who keep themselves at a distance from those they seek to lead rarely produce commitment which can only really come through personal relationships. Top executives who hide behind a senior management team and a large desk in a secluded office don't create loyalty. Deep attachments only stem from being able to share in the decision making processes. Jesus didn't make all the decisions. Sometimes he left it to his disciples to strike out on their own to heal the sick, cast out the demons and to preach the good news of the kingdom.

---

[69] John 15:15

In his humanity Jesus wisely recognised that there had to be limits on his time and energy and that he simply couldn't make every decision himself. So he began by appointing twelve to be with him and then a little later he brought in a further seventy others. Some of them proved to be ineffective, others doubted and failed him and a number even denied him altogether. Nevertheless Jesus knew that sharing the load was the only long-term route to success. He allowed his first team members to make their mistakes and learn from them as we read in the Book of Acts and elsewhere in the New Testament.

The following anonymous light-hearted piece illustrates something of the risk that Jesus took when he decided to share leadership with his twelve disciples!

Memorandum   **JMC**

To   Jesus, son of Joseph
          Woodcraft Carpenter Shop
          Nazareth

From   Jordan Management Consultants
          Jerusalem

Dear Sir,
Thank you for submitting the resumes of the twelve men you have picked for management positions in your new organisation. All of them have now taken our battery of tests; we have not only run the results through our computer, but also arranged personal interviews for each of them with our psychologist and vocational aptitude consultant.

It is our opinion that most of your nominees are lacking in background and vocational aptitude for the type of enterprise you are undertaking. They do not have the team concept. We would recommend that you continue your search for persons of experience in managerial ability and proven capability.

Simon Peter is emotionally unstable and given to fits of temper. Andrew has absolutely no qualities of leadership. The two brothers, James and John, the sons of Zebedee, place personal interest before company loyalty. Thomas demonstrates a questioning attitude that would tend to undermine morale. We feel that it is our duty to tell you that Matthew has been blacklisted by the Greater Jerusalem Better Business Bureau. James, the son of Alphaeus, and Thaddaeus definitely have radical leanings, and they both registered a high score on the manic-depressive scale.

One of the candidates, however, shows great potential. He is a man of ability and resourcefulness, meets people well, has a keen business mind and has contacts in high places. He is highly motivated, ambitious and responsible. We recommend Judas Iscariot as your controller and right-hand man. All the other profiles are self-explanatory.

We wish you every success in your new venture.

Sincerely yours,
Jordan Management Consultants

Compassionate and caring leadership

Leadership that attracts a committed following needs to be compassionate. People want to know their leader understands where they are coming from. They need someone who cares deeply about their issues and listens and acts on their concerns. We see this quality exemplified in the life of Jesus. The first century Roman poet, Horace, once wrote: 'How I hate the vulgar crowd'. But Jesus was different. He loved the crowds, and 'he was moved with compassion for their needs'. When the lepers came with their twisted and deformed limbs crying out 'unclean', 'unclean' to keep the people away from them, Jesus came and touched and cleansed them. When he encountered the sick and the mentally ill his heart went out to them and he rebuked their sicknesses and made them well. When people came with their fears and mental darkness he drove out their demons and when those who were stricken with guilt and loneliness came he brought forgiveness and friendship.

One day after Jesus had spent long hours teaching a large crowd by the Sea of Tiberius he was moved with compassion because he knew that most of them were very hungry. So, he told his disciples to make the people sit down and there followed a miracle in which five thousand hungry people were fed on five barley loaves and two small fish. It proved to be compassion of a most generous kind because John recorded that when they had all had enough to eat the disciples collected up twelve baskets full of fish and bread.

Occasionally we catch glimpses of this same compassionate leadership in some of the world's Christian leaders. William and Catherine Booth, the co-founders of the Salvation Army, felt deeply for the needs of the working poor in Victorian England. They were 'the submerged tenth', the men and women who worked for very low wages on a casual daily basis. They lived on the bread line in damp infested basements and draughty attics in London's East End. The Booths who responded to their needs were leaders driven to help by the compassion of Jesus. They set up rescue homes for prostitutes and started orphanages for homeless children. They established a missing person's bureau and a Household Salvage Brigade which would collect up useable, unwanted clothing, furniture, household goods and even edible food. The plan may perhaps have been over-paternalistic by today's standards but it was compassionate and it won over the hearts of many hundreds who lived a hand to mouth existence.

We see a reflection of divine compassion in John Wesley's leadership of the early Methodists. He vigorously opposed slavery, the insanitary conditions of the prisons, the dangers in factories and mines, the lack of care for the sick and the inadequacy of education for young children. A year before he died he recorded in his journal that he had waded knee deep in snow collecting food and blankets for the poor of Bristol. We see compassion in the tender, sensitive, gentle medical care of Dr David Livingstone. When the American journalist Henry Morton Stanley discovered him attending to the needs of the suffering tribal peoples of East Africa on the shores of Lake Tanganyika he became a Christian immediately without Livingstone even having spoken to him!

Servant ministry and being a servant requires humility, great patience and tolerance. Jesus' disciples James and John must have greatly disappointed him when they asked to have the top managerial positions in his kingdom. Once when the disciples reached the people of Samaria they were given a hostile reception. James and John wanted to call down fire on them. Needless to say Jesus restrained them and explained that this was not the way of his kingdom and that he had come to save lives not destroy them.[70]

On one particular occasion, just after Jesus had been warning about the dangers of getting captivated by material possessions, Peter said, 'We have left everything to be in this with you but what will we get out of it'? Once again Jesus had to explain that his kingdom is not a material kingdom.[71] Jesus' commitment was sometimes tested to the limits. While he hung dying on a cross all his disciples left him and fled. Even Peter who had vehemently asserted that he would never be a betrayer ended up denying any knowledge of him. Yet Jesus

---

[70] Luke 9:54
[71] Matthew 19 :27

appeared to them all after his resurrection and re-commissioned them. On the Day of Pentecost he empowered them with his Holy Spirit. Jesus' unswerving loyalty to his followers was a vital aspect of his effective leadership. Without this quality team building simply wasn't and isn't possible.

Jesus' compassionate care and practical action drew the people to 'hear him gladly'.[72] And it is still so! People to-day are still drawn to follow leaders who are men and women of compassion. Most obviously the Nelson Mandelas of this world. Jesus is the exemplary compassionate leader. His great parable was that the Good Samaritan's compassion for the man who was mugged by thieves is the role model for all his followers. The central figure and lesson of his parable of the Prodigal Son is the compassionate Father. It is this sacrificial love that binds people together.

Discerning Leadership

It is important that servant leaders are savvy and street-wise. Jesus urged all his followers to have their wits about them and know what's going on around them as well as in the world beyond. When Jesus sent his disciples out on their very first mission he told them 'to be as shrewd as snakes and as innocent as doves'.[73]

Jesus revealed his discernment on many occasions. When he first met Nathaniel he knew immediately that he was a person of integrity with no hidden agenda or dark side. He knew that Zacchaeus was a dishonest tax collector and he went to his home and urged him to repay immediately those he had cheated. Once on a particularly hot day Jesus sat down by the well in the Samaritan village of Sychar and asked a woman who was there for a drink.

[72] Mark 12:37
[73] Matthew 10:16

As they entered into a discussion the woman was captivated by Jesus' insights into her issues. Indeed she was totally amazed when he suddenly reminded her that she had been through five marriages and was now living with a man who was not her husband! She went into the centre of the village and told the people to come and see a man 'who told me everything I ever did'.

It's not simply discerning people's motives and agendas that are important. Good leaders assess issues wisely and rightly. They are men and women who can respond appropriately in a crisis. Jesus was not thrown off course by opposition from the religious leaders of his day, the Pharisees and Sadducees. When he was asked catch questions about marriage or paying taxes to Caesar he quickly spotted the traps. He pointed out that a man who had had seven wives in this life would not be polygamous in the next because there is no married state in the life to come. As for paying taxes to Caesar his astute reply was 'to give to Caesar what is justly Caesar's and to God what is God's'!

Integrity and leadership

Jesus was a leader whose personal life was one of total integrity. He knew the truth later expressed by Christian writer, Oswald Chambers, that 'our value to God in public is what we are in private'. He didn't engage in manipulative rhetoric. He was not caught up in any scandal. His words were always appropriate to the occasion. Sometimes there was righteous anger and rebuke. At other moments there was challenge or questioning. On many occasions he spoke words of healing, forgiveness and encouragement. Everyone was touched by his words which were always gracious, positive and affirming. Jesus never allowed popularity to run to his head. When the people came and tried to make him political king after he had fed five

five thousand hungry people he slipped away through the crowd. The only quality that he ever claimed for himself was that of humility. He said, 'Take my yoke upon you and learn from me, for I am gentle and humble in heart, and you will find rest for your souls'.[75]

Other facets of Jesus' leadership

There are many other facets of Jesus' leadership which it is not possible to recount in one small chapter. He knew that his kingdom mission was always a total assignment. It was all or nothing. In all his leadership Jesus displayed great courage. He loved his disciples and co-workers to the very end. He never gave up either on them or the task in hand despite great hostility. Jesus' leadership was one of great perseverance; 'He endured great opposition from sinful men and endured the cross and despised the shame'.[76]

Like all great leaders Jesus drew strength and encouragement from the lives of leaders who had gone before him. He often quoted from Moses and Abraham and was evidently impressed by the fortitude of Elijah, Elisha and John the Baptist. He also drew strength from the teachings of Isaiah.

Throughout his leading Jesus always looked forward with a positive outlook. He knew it was important to be flexible. If his team was persecuted in one place he moved them on elsewhere to a more receptive audience. He knew that his kingdom would triumph in the end and he confidently assured his disciples that he would see them again after his resurrection. Then he would send them out into the Roman Empire and the territories beyond as heralds of his kingdom.

---

[75] Matthew 11:29
[76] Hebrews 13:2

Jesus was ever a man of his word. His 'yes' was always 'yes' and his 'no' always 'no'.[77] This was something which Winston Churchill later recognised as crucial in any leader. 'There is', he said on one occasion, 'no worse mistake in public leadership than to hold out false hopes soon to be swept away'. On another occasion he said, 'You must never make a promise which you do not fulfil'.

Importantly Jesus was a leader who knew how to take care of himself. The pressures of demanding people were sometimes so great that he found himself too busy even to eat. But he knew the importance of self-care and straight away took time out to rest, pray and relax. Luke tells us 'Jesus often withdrew to lonely places and prayed'.[78] He also found renewed energy through visiting friends, sharing meals, walking out and delighting in the natural world around him. In short it is plain to see that Jesus set and modelled the very best pattern of leadership the world has ever seen. If evidence of that fact was ever needed it is that there are many more people in the world of today of all religions and none who still follow his leadership principles rather than anyone else's.

[77] Matthew 5:37
[78] Luke 5:16

CHAPTER 5
The Fact of Suffering

P robably the hardest issue we all of us have to face in our lives is the fact of suffering and pain. It's everywhere about us and no one can escape from it or its consequences. It is nevertheless the contention of this chapter that although Christianity doesn't offer a complete set of philosophical answers to the problem of suffering it does offer a present help when we suffer. This is quite simply because Jesus, the author of the Christian faith, not only experienced human suffering to the full but his presence in the lives of his followers sustains, strengthens and comforts them in their pain. Jesus, God and Saviour, became a human being and experienced earthly suffering to the very depths. When he left this world he did so as a man carrying with him his memories and experience of suffering. Today he is still man and still able to feel for us in our trials. As the apostle Paul put it in his *Letter to Timothy*, 'there is one mediator between God and men, the man Christ Jesus'.[79] So this chapter begins with a brief introduction to the nature and issues arising from suffering, but its focus is on showing the ways in which Jesus offers us a present help.

The Fact of Suffering

Suffering comes in many forms – physical, emotional and mental. It can be inflicted upon us by others, by human accident, by the environment or by our own attitude, words or actions. We are

---

[79] 1 Timothy 2:5

constantly aware of suffering in every aspect of this Earth. We see it in the natural world, in the animal kingdom and in human life and interaction. Although our planet is stunningly beautiful and rich in natural resources it also generates a great deal of devastation and hurt. We see it in earthquakes, tsunamis, flooding, avalanches, mud slides and volcanic eruptions. There are estimated to be an average of fifteen major earthquakes every year. One of the most destructive eruptions took place on 12th January 2010 in Haiti and resulted in 316,000 deaths. Tsunamis have been described as 'mother nature's worst nightmares'. At their most devastating they can move at the speed of a jet airliner. One of the most deadly struck Indonesia in 2018 with waves twenty feet high swamping the land and leaving 150,000 dead or missing. To this wanton destruction, can be added the fact that 2.3 billion people are estimated to have been devastatingly affected by floods in the past twenty years.

The loss of life caused by natural disasters bears no comparison to that brought about by human greed, selfishness and war. The Russian dictator, Joseph Stalin, murdered possibly as many as 20 million people in his revolutionary purges of the 1930s. In 1939 Adolph Hitler started a world war in which 60 million people died and that produced a holocaust in which six million Jews went to their death in concentration camps. This terrifyingly brutal genocide was followed by three million deaths that are known to have taken place in the 'killing fields' of Pol Pot. In 1994 more than one million Tutsis were put to death in Rwanda by Hutus using machetes and clubs. To this must be added the destruction and loss of life brought about by Saddam Hussein, Bassar Assad, Al-Qaeda, Isis and Boko Haram. Then there are mass shootings in the United States; 250 0f them in the first eight months of 2019. At the same time in the UK deaths from knife crime on the streets reached epidemic proportions. Millions of people across the world's continents have been displaced from their homes as a result of war and violence and now find themselves in refugee camps and lacking the most basic necessities of life. Other suffering we recognise is caused by human selfishness and carelessness. Trains passing red signals, vehicles breaking the speed limit, poor aircraft maintenance, lack of proper risk-assessments and a host of other bad decisions all result in death and destruction.

It isn't only pain resulting from violence that inflicts people. Vast numbers are starving and dying on account of diseases such as ebola, cholera and typhoid while others are terminally ill with cancers, heart attacks and respiratory diseases. Many in every part of the globe find themselves in acute physical, mental and emotional pain. Others suffer from dementia, experience the trauma of loss or find themselves in the grip of mental and moral darkness. In domestic life there appears to be growing violence and abuse, marital break-down and unwanted children. These brief references to human agony and pain in relatively recent times are only the tip of an iceberg of suffering stretching back to the beginning of time.

Suffering truly is, in the words of Epicurus, the third century Greek philosopher, 'the mystery of the universe'. Unsurprisingly when George Barna, the public opinion pollster, organised a survey based on the question, 'If you could ask God only one question what would you ask?, the most frequent response was, 'Why is there pain and suffering in the world'?

Suffering is not always easy to define. Most would probably agree that it is a level of pain or hurt which is hard to live with and that takes way our peace and the general feeling of well-being. Suffering of course is not necessarily always bad or as bad as we imagine. Sometimes it acts as a warning of danger. Chest pains or migraines may be a result of stress and act as a warning to slow down. Someone may have caused us great emotional pain by their plain straight-speaking but nevertheless have saved us from a disastrous relationship or making a wrong decision. A driving accident to a ninety-four year old prince was a warning that the time had come to surrender his license.

Christianity, a help in times of suffering

Jesus' life and teaching offers an understanding of suffering.

The Christian faith recognises that we live in a material world that is fundamentally good but at the same time impacted with evil. Human beings are not robots or automatons, they are born with the capacity to make choices. A great deal of this imperfection and suffering we see around us results from human selfishness and wrong decision making but there nevertheless remains suffering which cannot be attributed solely to ourselves. Christianity doesn't give comprehensive explanations as to why human pain exists on Earth in such magnitude. What it does offer is a God who didn't, and doesn't, stand aloof from suffering but in defiance of it became a human being in the person of Jesus. Jesus didn't passively resign himself to the suffering in the world. Rather in his humanity he tried always to redeem it and overcome it with his goodness. As the Russian philosopher Nicolai Berdyaev once put it, 'We can only reconcile ourselves to the tragedy of the world because God suffers too'.

Jesus can help us to respond positively in times of suffering. We may have to endure pain and hurt but he demonstrated that we can indeed learn from it and grow in character and his likeness through it. One of his apostles wrote, 'Although he was a son, he learned obedience from what he suffered and, once made perfect, he became the source of eternal salvation for all who obey him'.[80] Quintin Hogg, better known as Lord Hailsham, recounted in his autobiography how he had been able to make sense of suffering though reading '*The Book of Job*'. 'It is, he wrote', 'by far the most penetrating analysis of the meaning of suffering I have ever read, may be the most illuminating ever written, and the poetry and prayer in the psalms and other poetical books is something which has been the inspiration of Christians from the earliest days to the present'.

Jesus' Spirit in us brings wellness.

It is universally recognised that our emotional well-being impacts our physical well-being and that the root of physical pain and suffering can sometimes be for the reason that we are not at ease with ourselves or the world outside. Put another way physical disease or pain can spring from disease in our emotional lives. When once we have entrusted ourselves to Jesus and received his divine forgiveness for our selfishness, sin and wrong we discover that the past truly is behind us and that our 'consciences are cleansed from guilt'.[81] We also find a new and deep-rooted peace within ourselves. Knowing that we are loved, affirmed and accepted in this way as we are and for who we are, will enable us to feel more comfortable in our own skin. This in turn will help us to think and live more positively and hopefully. There is power in positive thinking. Healthful imagination exerts an invigorating impact on our well-being The Book of Proverbs counsels us, 'Above all else, guard your heart, for it is the wellspring of life'.[82] The apostle Paul reminds us that 'God is able to do immeasurably more than all we ask or imagine, according to his power that is at work in us'.[83]

---

[80] Hebrews 5:8-9
[81] Hebrews 10: 22
[82] Proverbs 4:23
[83] Ephesians 3: 26

Coming to faith in Jesus as God and Saviour is not an immediate short cut or easy guarantee we will overcome pain or illness or experience immediate healing though it is of course true that physical healing sometimes comes through praying. That said, down through the ages countless numbers of men and women have found that Jesus' presence enabled them to manage their pain and suffering with courage and perseverance.

Our character can be refined by Jesus through suffering

In addition to the peace and comfort of the Lord's presence there are other ways in which Jesus' presence helps us in times of suffering. Among them is the fact that our character can be refined and strengthened. James Barrie, the author of *Peter Pan*, once reflected on how his mother suffered the loss of the son she loved. 'That', he said, 'is how my mother got her soft eyes and that is why other mothers ran to her when they lost their child'. Suffering has the capacity to produce great strength and depth of character. The world witnessed this same truth in the life of Nelson Mandela when he emerged from twenty seven years of imprisonment on Robben Island.

This moulding and shaping of character through pain and suffering is something we see in Jesus himself. In his humanity 'Jesus learned obedience through the things that he suffered and, once made perfect, he became the source of eternal salvation for all who obey him'.[84] What was true of Jesus in his humanity is also true for his people. In his early days as Jesus' disciple Peter was often boastful and sometimes arrogant. On one occasion he forthrightly declared that even if all of Jesus followers were to desert him he certainly would never do so. However when Jesus was taken into custody on false charges Peter denied his Lord three times on the same morning before

---

[84] Hebrews 5:8-9

the cock crowed. Hannah More was once the doyenne of eighteenth century London society. Following her conversion and commitment to Christ she became a great social reformer and pioneer for the education of the poor. In one of her tracts she wrote that, 'Affliction is the school in which great virtues are acquired, in which great characters are formed. It is a kind of moral gymnasium, in which the disciples of Christ are trained to robust exercise, hardy exertion, and severe conflict'.

The apostle Peter wrote to encourage the persecuted and suffering Christians in Asia Minor. He began by telling them that 'the grief and various trials' they had been suffering had come about so that their faith which was of 'greater worth than gold might be proved genuine and bring praise, honour and glory to Jesus Christ.[85] His closing words to them were that after they had suffered 'Christ would make them strong, firm and steadfast'.[86] The apostle James similarly urged his readers to recognise that the trials they were facing would increase their perseverance so that they would be 'mature and complete'.[87] The way in which positive responses to suffering and pain transforms and builds character has been likened to the way in which the irritant inside an oyster gradually results in the making of a beautiful pearl'. Dr Billy Graham, the twentieth century evangelist, wrote: 'Some of the most godly people I've ever known were men and women who were called upon to endure great suffering. They could have grown bitter and resentful...yet, because they knew Christ and walked in the joy of His presence every day, God blessed them and turned them into people who reflected Christ'.

---

[85] 1 Peter 1; 6-7
[86] 1 Peter 5:10
[87] James 1:3-4

Jesus' example in suffering gives us courage in ours.

A twelfth century monk and theological teacher in Paris by the name of Peter Abelard began to remind people that Jesus' death was the ultimate act of love. At his cross Abelard wrote that we see the supreme example of sacrifice. He quoted from the Gospel of John chapter 15, 'Greater love has no-one than this that a man lay down his life for his friends'. 'God', Abelard explained, 'has fully bound us to Himself by love and so our hearts are enkindled by this gift of divine love'. Through the centuries following Abelard's time other Christian teachers also wrote of the inspiring example of Jesus' sacrificial love in what is sometimes referred to as the 'exemplarist' love of Jesus. And it is this inspiring example that has sustained many hundreds of individuals in times of pain, sickness and suffering.

The Letter to the Hebrews was addressed to Christians who were being tempted to throw in the sponge because they were suffering hostility and difficult times. The apostle urged them to consider and take encouragement from the example of Jesus. He wrote: 'Let us fix our eyes on Jesus the author and perfecter of our faith, who for the joy set before him endured the cross, scorning its shame and sat down on the throne of God. Consider him who endured such opposition from sinful men, so that you will not grow weary and lose heart'.[88] The key to overcoming our pain is to keep our focus on Jesus who overcame the agony of the cross and now gives us strength and help in our hour of need. Peter wrote to Christians in Asia Minor who 'suffered grief in all kinds of trials'[89] urging them to constantly draw strength from the exemplary courage of Jesus.

Jesus can speak through our suffering.

Paul suffered from what he described as 'a thorn in the flesh'. It's not clear precisely what this was but it was evidently some kind of

[88] Hebrews 12:2-3
[89] I Peter 1:6

ailment which caused him considerable pain. He prayed several times calling out to the Lord for healing and relief but nothing happened. Then at some point shortly afterwards he distinctly heard the Lord say; 'My strength is sufficient for you, for my power is made perfect in weakness'.[90] We don't know whether Paul heard a normal speaking voice or whether it was a prompting from within his spirit. The important thing was that he recognised that he was being too dependent on his own physical and emotional resources.

This is a common issue for many people. The world about us is full of very able and capable men and women who stretch themselves to the limits of their capacity and beyond. The result is their work life balance has gone, their judgements are impaired, their moral boundaries are crossed and their relationships are broken or perhaps even destroyed. Along with the apostle Paul people are often so busy that it sometimes takes physical sickness or the pain or even perhaps a major breakdown in our health to bring them back to reality. As St Augustine once put it, 'God wants to give us something, but cannot, because our hands are full – there's nowhere for him to put it'. The Lord in his concern may use our sufferings to speak to us if only we are sufficiently open to listen.

C.S. Lewis, the author of the Narnia books, expressed it so clearly in his book *The Problem of Pain*. He wrote:

> But pain insists on being listened to. God whispers to us in our pleasures, speaks to us in our conscience, but shouts to us in our pains, it is his megaphone to rouse a deaf world. A bad man, happy, is a man without the least inkling that his actions do not answer, that they are not in accordance with the laws of the universe.

Jesus presence in times of suffering can bring out the best in us

It is a fact that suffering and pain can have the effect of bringing out the very best in us. Why this should be is something of a puzzle.

---

[90] 2 Corinthians 12:9

It may be that pain some how causes the ultimate good in us to surface in our minds. This seems to have been true of John, one of Jesus' closest friends. In his later years he became a leader in the Christian church at Ephesus. Tradition has it that he was put in a vat of boiling oil but managed to survive. He was then banished to the Greek Island of Patmos by the Roman Emperor Domitian. There he spent much of his time chained to the walls of a cave which looked down over the harbour. Despite his bitter suffering he was able to set down in writing the wonderful visions of heaven which we now know as the Book of Revelation, the last book in the Bible.

We see in the life of George Frederick Handel the way in which inspiring beauty can be born of suffering. Towards the end of his days his fortunes and health were failing. His right side was paralysed and his money at an end. Seized and threatened by his creditors with imprisonment he was tempted to give up the fight. Then when it was almost too late he rediscovered the sustaining strength of Jesus and rebounded to compose his greatest music – 'The Messiah'. Out of his suffering came a work which has proclaimed the Christian message to millions. Handel's suffering resulted in the glory of God.

When David Livingstone the Scottish missionary and explorer returned home after sixteen years in Africa his body was emaciated by some twenty seven different fevers that he had suffered. His left arm which had been mauled by a lion hung useless at his side. In his address to the students at Glasgow University, he said that what had sustained him during his lonely exile was Jesus' promise, 'Lo I am with you always, even to the end of the age'.

Jesus empathises with us in our suffering

If someone we really love, perhaps a child, a relative or a close friend suffers sickness or severe pain, it often happens that we suffer with them. Indeed we may even feel pain or nausea our self. It's the same with Jesus. When his people experience illness or hurt He hurts with them. We see an instance of this when the early believers in Jerusalem were suffering great brutality at the hands of Saul the persecutor. The risen Lord confronted him on the road to Damascus with the words, 'Saul, Saul, why do you persecute *me*'?[91] In other words the risen Jesus actually felt as if he was being persecuted because his followers were being persecuted. From this the *Letter to Hebrews* encourages us with the fact that Jesus is therefore able to sympathise with us in our weaknesses. He is literally in our sufferings and we are in his suffering. The New Testament speaks of this as 'the fellowship of sharing in Christ's sufferings'.[92]

His word comforts and heals us in suffering

Many people who have suffered pain or severe illness have found that healing comes from reading, speaking or meditating on the words of the Bible. When my first wife Liz was dying of cancer she found great comfort and strength during her illness by speaking Scriptural affirmations and promises out loud. Sometimes I said them with her. Two of her very close friends used to visit her each week and read and shared from the Bible with her. Positive assertions lead to positive thinking and a positive mindset. The Old Testament Psalms encourage us to declare out aloud what God has done for us and to meditate on his word. In fact one of the meanings of the Hebrew word 'to meditate' is to talk aloud. This is a practice which has real benefits in helping us in times of suffering. It's important to remember that as Jesus was dying on the cross he was meditating aloud on Psalm 22 and other biblical passages.

Countless numbers of people suffering grief on account of losing a loved one have found great comfort in hearing Psalm 23

---

[91] Acts 9:4
[92] Philippians 3:10

'The Lord's My Shepherd' read or sung. There is something very similar to this expressed in Psalm 107. There the Psalmist is reflecting on various periods of suffering through which his people had passed during their history. Among other things they had passed through a time of severe sickness in the wilderness which had caused them 'to loathe any kind of food and drew them near to the gates of death'. Then 'when they cried out in their trouble', the Psalmist noted, 'the Lord sent forth his word and healed them'.[93]

Reading the accounts of Jesus' healing miracles and his care for the needy is a positive means of feeding our minds and emotions with fresh hope. I first realised this when I was the rector of four country parishes in the Anglican diocese of Montreal. It was a beautiful area in the Laurentian Mountains with lakes and forests where many wealthy people had second homes as summer retreats and bases for their winter skiing activities. The rectory garden ran down to the edge of a lake and had its own beach. During the summer vacation of 1972 a number of teenagers who had recently become Christians were doing their best to get free from the effects of the drugs they had been taking. They would sit in small groups on the grass between the church and the rectory which they referred to as 'Nige baby's pad' for days on end reading parts of the Bible out loud to each other. They found it was the best thing ever for recovering their minds!

Jesus calls us to overcome evil and suffering

Jesus didn't adopt a passive attitude to evil and suffering, he resisted it. His conflict in the wilderness at the beginning of his ministry was a direct confrontation with the evil. He resisted and overcame the devil and later disempowered the forces of darkness through his death on the cross. Jesus healed those who had been 'bound by Satan' and he cast out evil spirits. He taught his followers to

---
[93] Psalm 107:18-20

follow his example and overcome evil with good, allow his light to dispel the darkness and his love to take away fear and despair. Jesus' presence in us and the knowledge of his teaching will also help us to avoid the selfishness and carelessness which results in human pain and suffering. Instead of causing hurt his spirit in our lives will enable us to drive away hatred and anger.

In summary it is important to remind ourselves that as Christians we have a destiny to look forward to in a perfected world where there will no longer be any pain, sickness, crying or death. This is not a crutch or a fantasy but something promised by our Lord and God whose life and teachings are unequalled. Furthermore, the sufferings of this present world demand it and many of those who were in the process of dying have captured visions of it. Christianity offers a present help in suffering. In Jesus who is 'the true God and eternal life'[94] we have one who sustains us in our present suffering and destines us for a future without it.

---

[94] 1 John 5:20

CHAPTER 6
A Way Through Death

Everyone of us at some time has moments when we are anxious at the prospect of our death. Many people have deep fears about it and what might lie the other side of the grave. As we get older thoughts of death and planning for our death become more frequent. People differ greatly at the prospect of dying. Some are terrified. Some are weary and ready to go. Some are humanists - they believe that this life is all and that at the point of death there will be no further consciousness. All agree that death is indeed a major dilemma.

Here is what some well-known people have said about it. The Greek philosopher, Epicurus, regarded the unacknowledged fear of death as a primary cause of anxiety and once declared: 'The last thing I want to do is die. In regard to death everyone is a fortified city'. Henry VIII's Chancellor, Sir Thomas More, said during his trial before Thomas Cromwell in 1535, 'Death he comes for us all'. The eighteenth century French philosopher, Jean Jacques Rousseau' said: 'He who is afraid to face death without fear is a liar'. Voltaire, the French philosopher, spent a good deal of his life attacking organised religion and continued to do so at the time of his painful and agonising death. A priest visited him and asked if he wanted to return to the faith of his fathers and renounce the devil. He is alleged to have replied, 'This is no time to make new enemies' and to have cried out, 'I must die abandoned of God and man'. The nurse who attended him repeatedly said that 'for all the wealth of Europe she would never wish to see another infidel die. It was a scene of horror beyond exaggeration'.

Edward Gibbon, the English historian and author of *The History of the Decline and Fall of the Roman Empire*, said in his last words: 'All is now lost, finally and irrevocably lost. All is dark and doubtful'. Aldous Huxley, the twentieth century author of *Brave New World*, once wrote: 'If you are a busy chocolate eating modern, then death is hell'.

Even children think about death, perhaps even more than we realise. One of my eldest daughter's close friends told her that she had been out in the car and her little son was sitting in the back with his little cousin. Both of them were about four years old and were in their car booster seats. After a little while her small son said to his cousin, 'My grandpa's just died'. To which his cousin immediately replied, 'Who shot him then'? To which he replied, 'Nobody, he died his self'!

So these are some of the reasons which cause many people to try to hide away from the reality of death. If possible we avoid the actual word and speak instead of 'departing' or 'going to rest'. In fact we don't have 'a death service', we have an undertaker to take us under. We don't generally say, 'Mrs Williams has died' but rather 'Mrs Williams has passed away'. Rather than speak of 'the dead' we refer in gentler tones to 'our departed brother' or 'the late Mrs Smith'. When all is said and done however, death is the one certainty for us all. As Bernard Shaw once put it, 'Death is the ultimate statistic, 'One out of one dies'. It is however an issue to which the Christian faith has a clear answer and a future hope.

A founder who triumphed over death

Of all the founders of the world's major religions Jesus is unique in that he is the one who still lives. Gautama, Confucius, Muhammad, Guru Nanak and the founders of Hinduism are all figures of history who once lived and died. Their burial places are venerated shrines visited by the faithful. They are past history. But with Jesus it is not so. After his crucifixion he came alive again and indeed he continues to live. On the third day after his crucifixion he walked out of the rock hewn tomb in which he had been buried. He overcame death and showed himself alive to his followers over many days. Jesus very clearly taught that he would safely guide those whose trusted in him beyond the grave. One of his most unequivocal declarations was 'I am the resurrection and the life, he who believes in me shall never die'.[95]

Jesus the risen Lord.

Jesus overcame death and returned to be with his disciples for a period of forty days. He came alive in the very same body which was crucified and buried in the tomb belonging to Joseph who was a member of the Jewish Council and came from of Arimathea.[96] The disciples not only recognised him, they felt his wounds and touched the scars where the nails had passed through his hands and feet. Luke records in his gospel that Jesus said: 'Look at my hands and feet. It is I myself. Touch me and see; a ghost does not have flesh and blood as you see I have'.[97] This was no figment of the disciples' imagination because Jesus actually ate and drank with them. They were so stunned by his presence that Jesus asked them if they had anything to eat and they gave him a piece of cooked fish, and he took it and ate it in their presence.[98]

---

[95] John 11:25
[96] Luke 23:50-54
[97] Luke 24:37-39
[98] Luke 24:41-42

Clearly Jesus' resurrection was not a hallucination or some kind dream in the minds of the disciples, it was an objective historical 'out there' event. One of the Church of England's *Articles of Religion* entitled 'Of the Resurrection of Christ' sums the matter up very clearly as follows: 'Christ did truly rise again from death, and took again his body, with flesh, bones and all things appertaining to the perfection of Man's nature; wherewith he ascended into Heaven, and there sitteth, until he return to judge all Men at the last day'.

Evidence for Jesus' resurrection.

Jesus' victory over death and his resurrection are the central truths on which the whole of the Christian faith stands or falls. It is a stupendous claim that cannot be proved with absolute total certainty. Nevertheless there is very strong, sound, convincing and overwhelming evidence for it.

First and foremost it is plain to everyone that Jesus was dead and buried. Clearly there can't be a resurrection unless the person concerned has died. All the evidence is that Jesus was dead and buried. The gospels are unequivocal that when Jesus was taken down from the cross he was already dead. According to Mark's gospel, the Roman governor, Pilate, asked the soldiers to make sure that Jesus was dead.[99] John relates in his account of the burial that just to make matters absolutely sure one of the soldiers pierced Jesus' side with a spear which caused a sudden flow of blood and water.[100] Pilate then gave Jesus' body to Joseph of Arimathea who took it away and placed it in a tomb cut into a rock face. The entrance was sealed with a stone estimated by some to weigh more than a ton and just in case anyone who thought they were strong enough might be tempted to come and take the body away Pilate

---

[99] Mark 15:44-45
[100] John 20:34

ordered an armed guard to keep watch.[101] In view of this there was no way people could claim that Jesus wasn't fully dead and that he somehow managed to recover in the cold of the tomb and push away the stone which secured the entrance.

Another piece of evidence which testifies strongly to the bodily resurrection of Jesus is the fact that when Mary and the other women arrived at dawn on the first day of the week to anoint Jesus' body with spices they were astonished to find that the tomb was empty.[102] The stone had been rolled away from the entrance and there was no body anywhere to be seen.[103] All four gospels are unanimous that the tomb was empty. So the resurrection was clearly more than just a vivid experience in the minds of the disciples.[104] Something definite and objective had happened before any of them saw the risen Jesus. The tomb was empty. The women and the disciples could see that it was empty, the Roman soldiers affirmed that it was empty and the Jewish authorities believed it was empty.

Not only was the tomb empty but no-one was able to produce the body of Jesus dead or alive. The Jewish Council would have done anything to have had possession of Jesus' corpse because that would have been the end of his movement. Likewise the Roman authorities would have been equally gratified to have been able to put an end to the matter but neither they nor the Jews were able to produce Jesus' body dead or alive.

A further and interesting piece of evidence is the grave clothes which Joseph of Arimathea had wrapped around Jesus' body when he took it down from the cross.[105] The gospel writer records that Simon Peter and John both ran to the empty tomb. When they arrived Peter

---

[101] Matthew 27:60
[102] Luke 24:2
[103] Matthew 28:2; Mark 16:4; Luke 24:2
[104] See especially 1 Corinthians 15:6
[105] John 19:38-40

went in first and 'saw the strips of linen lying there as well as the
burial cloth that had been around Jesus' head'. The cloth was folded
up by itself, 'separate from the linen'. John also went inside and he
'saw and believed'. What convinced him was that Jesus had
somehow emerged from the burial cloths perhaps in a manner akin
to that of a butterfly emerging from a cocoon.[106]

Supremely of course there is the evidence of the resurrection
appearances. The disciples walked and talked with the risen Jesus
and they ate and drank with him.[107] They fished with him and he
cooked food for them on the beach.[108] They saw the scars where the
nails had pierced his hands and feet and doubting Thomas was later
able to thrust his hand into Jesus' side.[109] The resurrection
appearances also have a ring of authenticity to them. Who writing a
fabricated account in the first century would have portrayed women
as the first witnesses to proclaim the risen Christ?[110] Jesus, we're
told, appeared to his disciples in a variety of different places and
circumstances. He appeared to Mary Magdalene at the tomb. He
met with the eleven disciples while they were eating and he broke
bread with Cleopas and his companion in the village of Emmaus.[111]
Very importantly the risen Jesus also appeared to Paul on the
Damascus Road and the once persecutor of the Christians became
the great apostle and missionary to the gentiles of the Roman
Empire.[112] Paul later wrote in his *Letter to the Corinthians* that the
risen Lord had appeared to more than five hundred of the brothers at
the same time, most of whom were still living.[113] Luke recorded at
the beginning of the *Book of Acts* that after his resurrection and over

---

[106] John 20:3-9
[107] Luke 24:41-42
[108] John 21:10-12
[109] John 21:27
[110] Matthew 28:1; Luke 24:9-10; John 20:1
[111] Luke 24:13-35
[112] Acts 9:1-6
[113] 1 Corinthians 15:6

a period of forty days Jesus showed himself to the apostles and 'gave many convincing proofs that he was alive'.[114] Also during this period he gave them teaching about the kingdom of God and told them not to leave Jerusalem until they had received the help and power of the Holy Spirit.

A number of scholars have highlighted the obvious fact that the sudden growth of the early Christian church and its rapid expansion can only be explained by the resurrection of Jesus. It is argued that a deceased unlettered carpenter from a small village in Judaea would not have been sufficient to account for the world-wide growth of Christianity. There is also the fact of the New Testament. It is equally difficult to imagine that the New Testament could have been written and copied and circulated so widely and in such quantity if Jesus had not risen from the dead.

That Sunday became the day of worship for the early Christians is very remarkable since the Jews were fanatically attached to the seventh day as the day of rest and worship. The fact of the matter was that the Jewish followers of Jesus changed their day of worship from the Seventh day Sabbath to the first day of the week in celebration of Jesus' resurrection. So for the early Christians every Sunday became a celebration of the risen Lord.

Perhaps we should also include the fact that there is even non-Christian evidence for the resurrection of Jesus. Josephus, a first century Jewish historian who remained a practising Jew and was hostile towards the Christians, wrote in his *History of the Jewish Nation*.

> Now there was about this time Jesus, a wise man, if it be lawful to call him a man, for he was a doer of wonderful works, a teacher of such men as receive the truth with pleasure. He drew over to him both many of the Jews, and many of the Gentiles. He was the Christ, and when Pilate,

[114] Acts 1:3

at the suggestion of the principal men among us, had condemned him to the cross, those that loved him at the first did not forsake him; for he appeared to them alive again the third day; as the divine prophets had foretold these and ten thousand other wonderful things concerning him. And the tribe of Christians so named from him are not extinct at this day.

This is a remarkable testimony which appears in the part of Josephus' text which scholars believe to be reliable and untampered with.

In the end possibly the greatest evidence of Jesus' resurrection is found in the changed lives of the first disciples who received his Spirit into their lives on the Day of Pentecost. At the time of Jesus' crucifixion they all of them left Jerusalem in fear with the exception of John who stood with Jesus' mother at the foot of the cross. Peter, 'the rock', denied Jesus three times. Yet within a matter of weeks he was boldly preaching Jesus to the crowds who had come to Jerusalem for the feast of Pentecost.[115] A short time later Peter and John brought healing to a man who was lame from birth and had been lying by one of the temple gates. As a result the Jewish religious leaders had the two disciples arrested for proclaiming the resurrection of Jesus and forbade them from doing any further such teaching. Peter and John's response was, 'Judge for yourselves whether it is right in God's sight to obey you rather than God. For we cannot help speaking about what we have seen and heard'. It was small wonder that the temple officials were astonished at their courage.[116]

But it wasn't only Peter and John whose lives were revolutionised by the presence of their risen Lord, all of the disciples were transformed from fear into bold and fervent witnesses for their Lord and all eventually died bravely for their faith in the risen Jesus. Early Christian traditions record that Matthew suffered martyrdom by the sword in Ethiopia. Mark died

---

[115] See Acts 2:14-41
[116] Acts 4:18-20

after being dragged through the streets of Alexandria. Luke was hanged on a tree in Greece. John was plunged into a cauldron of boiling oil but escaped death only to be banished to the mines in the island of Patmos. After having brought many of the inhabitants to faith in Christ he was taken back to Asia Minor where he died as an old man, the only apostle to have a peaceful death.

Peter was crucified at Rome with his head downwards. James-the-Great, John's brother, was beheaded at the command of King Herod Agrippa in Jerusalem in AD 44. James-the-Less, the son of Alphaeus, was thrown from a pinnacle of the temple and beaten to death on the ground below. Philip was hanged in Phrygia. James, the brother of the Lord, only became a committed believer after the risen Jesus had appeared to him. He then took on the role as leader of the Church in Jerusalem and later presided over the Council which met to consider the necessary requirements for those Gentiles who wanted to become members of the Christian church. He suffered martyrdom in AD 61 by stoning at the behest of the high priest Ananus. Bartholomew, also known as Nathanael, was flayed alive after preaching in Armenia. Andrew was crucified in Greece. Thomas was killed with a spear at Coromandel in India. Jude, also known as Thaddaeus, was shot to death with arrows. Matthias was first stoned and then beheaded, Simon was sawn in two while still alive. Barnabas suffered death by stoning at the hands of the Jews in Salonica.

So it is clear that the evidence that Jesus overcame death is solid. Indeed there are many people who, like Josephus, make no profession of faith but nevertheless believe that Jesus overcame death and appeared alive to his first followers.

Jesus offers himself not a teaching

Because Jesus triumphed over death he offers all who follow him not a teaching about the resurrection but himself who is the resurrection. This is vital because in the moment of our death our immediate need is not teaching about the resurrection but someone to call out to who can carry us safely through.

Many first century Jews were convinced believers in the resurrection. Their leaders, the Pharisees, frequently taught about the life after death. Their concept of a general resurrection had developed in the four hundred years before the coming of Jesus. We catch glimpses of it in the prophecy of Daniel and some of the Psalms. The Pharisees said that in the moment of death the two worlds of time and eternity met and kissed. Martha and her sister Mary were among Jesus' closest friends. Martha was a dedicated Jewess who held strongly to the orthodox teaching about the life after death given by the Pharisees. It doesn't however seem to have given her a great deal of comfort. When their brother Lazarus died she and her sister, Mary, sent for Jesus. On his arrival at the scene she confidently exclaimed of her brother, Lazarus, 'I know he will rise again in the resurrection at the last day'.[117] Immediately she had said this, Jesus looked at her and said: 'I am the resurrection and the life. He who believes in me will live, even though he dies; and whoever lives and believes in me will never die, Do you believe this'?.[118] In the face of death Jesus didn't offer her a teaching; he offered himself. He didn't say, as so many of the Pharisees did, 'I teach resurrection and life' but rather 'I am the resurrection and the life. He who believes in me shall never die'.[119] Then, almost without a pause he said to Martha, 'Do you believe this'? Her reply was highly significant, 'Yes Lord, I believe *you*'! 'I don't understand all the things you teach but I believe you'.[120]

---

[117] John 11:24
[118] John 11:25
[119] John 11:25-26
[120] John 11:27

This is the great Christian hope. Death is still an unknown but we know that Jesus has conquered it, and we have faith that if we cling to him in trust He will bring us safely through to an existence of total perfection. There is a legend about a man who was trapped and dying in some quick sands. It's doubtless a caricature, but like most caricatures it contains an element of truth. Confucius saw the man and remarked, 'There is evidence that men should stay away from such places'! Buddha came and said, 'Let that life be a lesson to the rest of the world'. Mohammed commented, 'Alas! It is the will of Allah'. A Hindu said, 'Never mind, you will return to earth in another form'. But when Jesus saw him, he said: 'Give me your hand brother, and I will pull you out'.

Death could be likened to going into a tunnel. As we make our entry we cling on to Jesus in faith and trust and he carries us through and out the other side into the perfect beyond. The apostle Paul writing to his young fellow worker Timothy put it this way, 'Our Saviour Jesus Christ has abolished death and brought life and immortality to light through the gospel'.[121] So our hope in death is not in a teaching but in a person, Jesus, the one who overcame death.

We may fear the process of dying but if our trust is in Jesus, 'Our Great God and Saviour' there is no ultimate reason to fear. Dr Martin Luther King who campaigned so hard for equal rights for Black people in America had an almost constant stream of death threats on his life. Someone once asked him if he was afraid of dying? He replied that he wasn't because he had been to the mountain. What he meant by that was he had spent time alone in the presence of Jesus and entrusted his whole life into his care. If he died so be it. He knew the next moment he would be in the presence of Jesus the living God. Martha's faith likewise is crucial, 'Yes Lord', she says, 'I believe You'. Our faith in the face of death is not in a subjective experience of peace or calm

---

that we feel within ourselves, and that has its place, but it's in the objective presence of the Lord who overcame death and stands outside of us to guide us through.

Through the passage of time countless people have spoken of death as though it were the end. One means of understanding Jesus' overcoming it is the way in which many medieval sailors sought to find a sea passage round the southern tip of the African continent. During the course of the Middle Ages many Europeans were strongly of the view that there was a way round the Southern tip of Africa and on to India and the far East. However all attempts to round the Cape proved to be of no avail. In fact it became known as the 'Cape of Storms' because so many sailors died in shipwrecks there. Eventually one brave mariner determined to try yet again. This man successfully rounded Southern Africa and reached the land of the spices later sailing back with a rich cargo of treasures to prove it. Ever since Vasco da Gama returned to his native Portugal in triumph it has been impossible to doubt that there is a way through the seas at southern tip of Africa. In fact because of Da Gama's heroic feat the very name 'Cape of Storms' was changed to the 'Cape of Good Hope'. This historical event mirrors what Jesus accomplished in regards to death. By dying and then returning alive he has demonstrated that there is a way through death. In reality Jesus has changed death from being a 'Cape of Storms' into a 'Cape of Good Hope'.

But there's more! Not only does Jesus carry his people through death he brings them to an existence where there is 'no more death or mourning or crying or pain',[122] in short to heaven. This great future hope is considered in chapter 7.

---

[122] Revelation 21:4

A hope beyond death

Aristotle, the Greek philosopher, said, 'Death is a dreadful thing for it is the end'. Thomas Hobbes, the seventeenth century English philosopher, said of the prospect of death, 'I leap into the dark'. Bertrand Russell wrote in his book *Why I am not a Christian*, 'I believe that when I die I rot, and nothing of my ego will survive'. So many people speak in these same terms as though death were the end. What a sad ending for Mr Jones that he should have to go like that. Old Fred believed this life is all and when you die that's it - finished. This is doubtless how it seemed to most of the crowd when Jesus came to the grave of Lazarus. Just another sad ending!

However when everything appeared to be at an end, Jesus reminded them that death is only the end of the beginning. It's the gateway into a much larger and perfect sphere of life in which 'whoever lives believing in me shall never die'. To underline this claim that he truly is the resurrection and the life, Jesus then performed his greatest miracle and raised Lazarus who had been dead for four days back to life.[123] Jesus stood before the tomb and called in a loud voice, 'Lazarus come out'. He did just that and struggled out of the tomb still wrapped and tangled with the burial cloths.

As Christians we may perhaps fear the process of dying and that is very understandable especially if the person concerned is suffering a painful illness. But we've no need to fear death itself because Jesus' power will transform our bodies and raise them up to a new beginning. The last reported words of Edward the Confessor, King of England, were, 'weep not I shall not die; as I leave the land of the dying I trust to see the blessings of the Lord in the land of the living'. Edward the Confessor was right. We call this world 'the land of the living' but in reality it is 'the land of the dying'. William Barclay rightly stated that 'through Jesus Christ we know that when death comes we do not pass

---

[123] John 11: 17 and 39

out of the land of the living: we pass into the land of the living'. The straightforward Christianity of Jesus is that death is not something to be feared. Rather it is the gateway to something far more wonderful. It is in the words of Augustine 'the end which is no end'.

Jesus brings comfort in bereavement

The death of someone we love or even a close neighbour or work colleague can cause us deep grief and sadness. In fact a person's death is often hardest for the loved ones who are left behind. According to the beginning of chapter 11 of the *Gospel of John* when Lazarus was seriously ill Mary and Martha sent word to Jesus to come to their house. They knew that above all Jesus was someone they could turn to for help. Even when Jesus wasn't able to make it to Bethany before Lazarus had died they still urgently wanted him to come and bring the comfort and strength of his presence. When at last Jesus reached the grave side and saw Mary weeping, he too wept deeply.[124] Jesus entered into the grief of the two sisters and their family and friends.

Jesus is the Almighty God who can speak life into the dead but He is also 'the man of sorrows who is acquainted with grief'. He is the Good Shepherd who walks with us 'through the Valley of the shadow of death' and 'comforts us with his rod and staff'. Jesus is never nearer than when we ourselves are in sorrow or need. He is as St Paul tells us 'the God of all Comfort'.[125] There is wonderful consoling and comforting power in the presence of the risen Lord. John Newton, a slave trading sea captain in the years before his conversion to Christ, expressed it so well in his hymn *How sweet the name of Jesus Sounds.*

---

[124] John 11:35
[125] 2 Corinthians 1:3

How sweet the name of Jesus sounds
In a believer's ear
It sooths his sorrows, heals his wounds
And drives away his fear.

The eighteenth century revivalist Charles Wesley also expressed it in his great hymn, *'Jesus the name high over all'.*

Jesus the name the name that charms our fears
That bids our sorrows cease
Tis music in the sinner's ears
Tis life and health and peace.

Jesus is truly the Lord who offers the way through death. He is truly the Lord who can carry us through death. It seems very relevant to bring this chapter to an end by recounting the death of Pope John Paul II. I have been to Rome eighteen times mostly with groups of students. One of my most memorable visits was in April, 2005. John Paul had been seriously unwell for some time but could have opted to have specialist hospital treatment. Many did their best to persuade him to do so. In the event however he refused because he felt that he had come to the end of his earthly life and he was confident that Jesus was calling him onwards and homewards. One of the very positive messages which came out of what was said at the time to have been the largest funeral in world history was that it caused people to focus on the ultimate purpose of life and the future resurrection hope that comes through Christ. Pope John Paul's last words before he died were, 'Let me go to the house of my Father'. During an earlier occasion at a huge Mass in Warsaw, soon after he had become Pope, he had been similarly forthright. Many people at that time had come to central square in the heart of the city in fear of the Communist authorities and apprehensive as to what might lie ahead but Pope John Paul said in his address, 'My dear people don't be afraid , throw open your doors to Jesus'. In the moment of our death we who are the followers of Jesus can indeed 'throw open our doors' to Him in the knowledge that He is in indeed the safe way through death who will carry us through to life in all its fullness.

CHAPTER 7
A Future Hope

O ne of the qualities which sustains us on our journey through life is hope. We a need present hope to keep us going and to see us through each day. We also need a future hope that this life won't simply come to a sad or an abrupt end but rather that it is a prelude to something far more wonderful, indeed perfection. This is in truth precisely what the Christian faith offers us. Hope is one of the great virtues. It means a continual and confident looking forward to the eternal world of perfection.

There are those who put down a belief in a future heaven as a form of escapism or wishful thinking. George Orwell did so in his novel *Animal Farm* where Moses, the raven, claimed to know of the existence of a mysterious country situated up in the sky called Sugar Candy Mountain to which all animals went when they died. Despite the fact that clover was in season there all the year round and lump sugar and linseed cake grew on the hedges most of the other animals on the farm were not impressed. Prominent among those who regard a future life of bliss as false hope was Karl Marx. He viewed heaven as a construct created to sustain the poor and the toiling working classes to enable them to cope with the misery and suffering of the nineteenth century industrial revolution.

The accusation that belief in a life to come is a form of escapism is easily countered. We have merely to consider the many Christian men and women who strongly believed in a future heaven but at the same time did so much to improve the conditions of the present world. We have only to think of Christians such as William Wilberforce who overcame the slave trade, or Elizabeth Fry who reformed the prisons, or the Salvation Army known through out the world for their passionate care. Florence Nightingale transformed nursing and played a major part in the introduction of formal training for nurses in Britain. Martin Luther King fought for racial equality in America, Mother Teresa cared for the dying on the streets of Calcutta, Nelson Mandela brought reconciliation to South Africa. Christian men and women pioneered education, founded colleges and Universities, built Missionary hospitals and led peace movements.

The Christian belief is that in the moment of death the spirit or self-conscious core that is within us, both linked to our bodies and yet distinct, leaves our human frame and enters into the divine presence. Jesus made this plain to the thief who was crucified alongside him when he said, 'Today you will be with me in paradise'. As Jesus himself hung on the cross he called out, 'Father into your hands I give my spirit'. The *Letter to the Hebrews* also speaks of 'the spirits of the just being made perfect'. The apostle Paul explained to the churches in Thessalonica[126] that, 'according to the Lord's own words', he will finally and decisively return at the close of the present world order. Then at that moment those who have died trusting in him will immediately be in his presence followed by those believers who are still alive on Earth. Writing to the Church in Corinth Paul states that in that very moment we will all be changed and our perishable bodies will be transformed into imperishable and immortal bodies.[127] The apostle John wrote that when Jesus appears at the end of the present age 'we shall be like him for we shall see him as he is'.[128]

---

[126] 1 Thessalonians 4: 15-16
[127] 1 Corinthians 15:52-54
[128] 1 John 3:2

Hard wired for heaven

From the earliest times down through the ages men and women have had visions of a future where the injustices and the pain of the present world order are righted. The early Hindu Vedas (scriptures) present us with a vision of *Svargan* which is a pleasure orientated world in which beings experience unlimited delight and where there is no pain and no death. For the Buddhists heaven is *Nirvana*, an experience of perfect peace and happiness in which selfish desire has been eliminated. In Islam heaven is depicted as *Jasinah*, a beautiful paradisal garden, a concept which Mohammed probably developed from his reading of the Old Testament.

So we could go on. In more recent times others have had visions of Beulah lands, Eldorados, Arcadias and perfected societies. Among the most famous are Thomas More's *Utopia* which he published in 1516 and John Milton's *Paradise Regained* published in 1671. Then at the beginning of the twentieth century J.M. Barrie published his novel *Peter Pan*. It features *Never Never Land*, a fictional island where Peter Pan, Tinkerbell, the Lost Boys and other mythical beings live. It's a place where people are immortal and don't grow up. Nowadays *Never Never Land* has become a metaphor for a future dream land.

Still to this day many people who suffer pain and loss dream of a *Never Never Land* or even perhaps of 'a sweet chariot coming for to take them home'. So why is this? Why do people, even those without any kind of religious belief, dream of a blissful future? The answer is for a variety of reasons. Plato, the Greek philosopher, taught that in the invisible world there exists the perfect form or idea of everything upon earth and that things on earth are shadowy imperfect copies of the heavenly unseen realities. So the reason, he suggested, why we have ideas of a perfect world is because somewhere beyond perfection and perfect relationships do actually exist.

C.S. Lewis, the author of the Narnia books, wrote along very similar lines. He made the point that 'creatures are not born with desires unless satisfaction for those desires can be met'. A baby for instance feels hunger and there is such a thing as food. A duckling wants to swim and there is such a thing as water. People have sexual desire and there is such a thing as sex. Lewis summed up his point in the following lines.

> If I find in myself a desire which no experience in this world can satisfy, the most probable explanation is that I was made for another world. If none of my earthly pleasures satisfy it, that does not prove that the universe is a fraud. Probably earthly pleasures were never meant to satisfy it, but only to arouse it, to suggest the real thing.

Others have argued that the injustices, inequalities and imperfections of the present world demand a future existence where justice, equality and perfection are complete. Speaking in September, 1942 Churchill urged that 'only faith in a life after death and a brighter world where dear ones will meet again – only that and the measured tramp of time can give consolation'.

So what is heaven like !

All this brings us to consider what is the nature of the Christian hope? What will it be like? Here of course care is needed as we come to interpret biblical texts and passages. Jesus in his humanity and the apostles are expressing what is unseen and beyond anything we have ever experienced. This means that we are dealing with metaphors, symbolism and picture language and we need to guard against over-literalising what we read. Gold applied to heaven for example simply represents splendour and eternity while music speaks of joy and ecstasy. It simply isn't possible to fully express what is unseen and perfect with visible and limited words. That is why the great apostle Paul once wrote, 'Eye has not seen, nor ear heard, neither has it entered the heart of men what good things God has prepared for those who love him'.[129] So what can we know about the nature of the Christian future hope?

An earthly paradise

John, who seems to have been the apostle closest to Jesus, was exiled on the Greek island of Patmos by Domitian who was the Roman emperor from AD 81-96. At some point, probably towards the end of this time, John had an overwhelmingly powerful encounter with the risen Jesus who gave him a series of visions of heaven. The most obvious and predominant aspect of them was of an earthly paradise. John wrote, 'I saw a new heaven and a new earth and the first heaven and the first earth had passed away. I saw the Holy City, the new Jerusalem, coming down out of heaven from God'.[130] Heaven is presented to us here as a perfected version of the most beautiful earthly existence imaginable. It is a place, Jesus said, 'where moth and rust do not destroy'.

This vision of a beautifully lighted and perfectly shaped walled city speaks of protection and lasting security. It's a hope which also finds echoes in the Old Testament where the great prophet Isaiah held out the hope of a new heaven and a new earth and of Jerusalem becoming a place where the sound of weeping and crying will be heard no more.[131] In chapter 21 of *Revelation* John also sees other perfected earthly aspects of heaven. The city has gates of pearl and streets and walls of pure gold. This speaks of exquisite beauty and security. At the beginning of *Revelation* chapter 22 we have the picture of 'the river of the water of life' and fruit bearing trees. Earlier

---

[129] Revelation 21:1-2
[130] Matthew 6:19
[131] Isaiah 65:17-19

in *Revelation* chapter 7 heaven is depicted as a place without hunger, thirst, pain or hurt where the deepest longings are satisfied. The apostle John's vision is very much what we should expect. After all he was a Jew and right from the beginning Genesis, the first Old Testament book, emphasises that when the world was made 'it was very good'. In the time of the great prophets Isaiah and Ezekiel every exiled Jew longed to return to a renewed and perfect Jerusalem.

All this emphasis is entirely in keeping with what Jesus taught about heaven. In chapter 14 of John's gospel for example Jesus told all who followed him not to be afraid of dying because 'in my Father's house there are many rooms' and that he has prepared a place for his followers. The Greek word which Jesus used for 'place' is often used to denote a physical locality. Jesus also spoke of there being a future heavenly banquet. At the conclusion of the Last Supper he told his disciples that he looked forward to drinking wine with them new in the kingdom of God. He was also clear that those who had made material sacrifices in this world would receive material rewards in the future.

Fully knowing the presence of God

In his vision John heard a loud voice saying, 'Now the dwelling of God is with men, and he will live with them. They will be his people and God himself will be with them and be their God'.[132] Here in this present busy world a Christian's relationship and experience of Jesus' presence is intermittent. Much depends on our outward circumstances at any given time and also our own physical and spiritual wellbeing. Jesus' presence often seems far away particularly if our life is an uphill struggle or we are in sickness or pain. The apostle Paul wrote in his famous hymn of love in his *Letter to the Corinthians* that now in this present life we only know

---

[132] Revelation 21:3

God in part but when the perfection of heaven comes 'then we will know him face to face'.[133] Saint Augustine, the fifth century North African bishop, could only express this in the following line, 'We shall see him, we shall love him, we shall praise him in the end which is no end'. So here it is clear that a central aspect of heaven is to fully experience the divine presence of Jesus, 'our great God and Saviour',[134] knowing that we are his people and that we belong to him.

In the present time we tend to think and experience Jesus as the man and the friend who walks along side of us and his people on our journeys through life. But in the new heaven and the new earth every person will be bathed in the light and the glory and the majesty of the risen Jesus who is seated on the throne depicting of course his supreme rule and authority. While those in heaven may be in awe and reverence of him there will not be fear or dread since heaven will be perfection in every way. In fact there is a touchingly tender note in the Book of Revelation where John sees 'God wiping away every tear from their eyes'.[135] In the very same passage comes the reminder that the risen Lord is 'trustworthy and true'. He will always be there to turn to and bring us hope no matter what.

The heart and centre of the Christian's future hope is the risen Jesus, the King of Kings and Lord of Lords. His light and splendour will shine down on the people of God who will be filled with the love and joy of his presence. The life and perfection of heaven will satisfy every need and longing symbolised by there being neither hunger nor thirst.

Freedom from pain and suffering

It is a mystery why people should suffer terrible diseases and be brutally treated, disabled in war or drowned in floods and buried

---

[133] 1 Corinthians 13: 12
[134] Titus 2:13
[135] Revelation 21:4

under earth-quakes or avalanches. It is hard even to contemplate killing fields, holocausts, genocides, chemical warfare and Britain and America selling weapons of war which lead to widespread destruction and loss of life. It's no wonder that philosophers have called suffering 'the mystery of the universe'. At the time John was writing out his visions of heaven Christian believers were being brutally treated by tyrannical Roman emperors and provincial governors. Every citizen in the empire was required to appear once a year before the magistrate, offer a pinch of incense and publicly swear 'Caesar is Lord'. Many Christians refused because for them Jesus was their Lord and, as is well-known, a great many were put to death.

Jesus came to show the world a better way. He fully experienced the pain and evil of our suffering world and brought forgiveness and peace to all who would turn to him. He urged his disciples not to be fearful or troubled but to find help and consolation in a future free of pain and hurt. He was going ahead to prepare a place for his followers, a place of security with many rooms. He also, as we have already noted spoke of heaven as a paradisal garden and place of joy and happiness. In the vision of heaven which John received from the Lord on the island of Patmos there was 'no more death or mourning or crying or pain, for the old order of things has passed away'. The risen Jesus was unequivocal that all the evils of the present world order were eternally banished. The cowardly, the unbelieving, the vile, the murderers, the sexually immoral, those who practice magic arts, the idolaters and liars will be summarily excluded.[136] Richard Baxter, the seventeenth century Puritan Pastor at Kidderminster expressed this freedom from suffering in the following lines.

There are none of those waves in the harbour which now so toss us up and down. Today we are well, tomorrow we are sick; today in esteem, tomorrow in disgrace; today we

---

[136] Revelation 21: 4&8

have friends, tomorrow we have none; nay we have wine and vinegar in the same cup...But there is none of this inconsistency in heaven. If perfect love casteth out fear, then perfect joy must needs cast out sorrow, and perfect happiness exclude all relics of misery. We shall there rest from all the evil of sin and of suffering.

The apostle Paul reminded the Corinthian church of teaching he had received directly from the Lord that in the future resurrection life of heaven bodies will be raised recognisable, glorious, perfect and imperishable. This means there will be no more selfishness, competitiveness, hatred or wrong. In short, all relationships will be perfected. In just the same way that Jesus was recognised by his disciples after his resurrection, so God's people will be recognisable in their resurrection bodies. In this there is further hope, comfort and consolation. In fact John ends his *Book of Revelation* with a vision of healing of the nations.[137]

John Bunyan expressed these three great aspects of heaven so beautifully at the end of Part 1 of *The Pilgrim's Progress*. Just as Christian was about to enter the 'Celestial City' he was met by two angels who said:

The heavenly Jerusalem you are now going to is the Paradise of God, wherein you shall see the Tree of Life and eat of the never fading fruits thereof...your walk and talk will be every day with the King, even all the days of eternity. There you shall not see again such things as you saw when you were in the lower region of the earth, to wit, sorrow, sickness, affliction and death, for *the former things are passed away*...You must there receive the comfort of all your toil, and have joy in all your sorrow...There you shall enjoy your friends again, that are gone thither before you; and there you shall with joy receive, even everyone that follows into the holy place after you. There you shall be clothed with glory and majesty, and put into an equipage fit to ride out with the King of Glory.

[137] Revelation 22:2

There is great positivity and consolation in the Christian hope of a perfect heaven beyond the grave. It is entirely reasonable to think that the injustices of the present world order demand it. Our inner spirits yearn for it. People who have had near death or short death experiences have captured glimpses of it. Jesus taught it. And the time is set when He, the risen Lord, the Alpha and the Omega, the beginning and the end, will make all things new.[138] A great encouragement in all of this is that the presence of Jesus is within the lives of all who follow him and this gives daily hopefulness. Indeed Jesus is described by Paul as 'our hope'[139] and by Peter as the one who 'has given us new birth into a living hope'.[140] Our ultimate hope as Christians is to fully know Jesus who is 'the true God and eternal life'[141] and, what is more, we can be strengthened in this hope because he is with us each step of the way throughout our life's journey.

---

[138] Revelation 22:5-6
[139] 1 Timothy 1:1
[140] 1 Peter 1: 3
[141] 1 John 5:20

CHAPTER 8
A Straight-forward Faith

Perhaps having read these chapters you may feel able to acknowledge Jesus, as his doubting disciple Thomas eventually did, and say, 'My Lord and my God'. To make such a declaration is to acknowledge that Jesus Christ is indeed the God of the universe who became a human being and lived among the people of this world in order to draw them back to himself. If this is where you're at, you are now in a position where you could become a straight-forward follower of Jesus. All that is needed is 'your unequivocal "yes" to Jesus'. 'Yes Lord Jesus I need you'. 'Yes Lord I need your forgiveness for my past' and 'Yes Lord I need your strength and help to live in the way I know I should in the future'. 'Yes Jesus I welcome your presence into my life this very moment'. 'Come Lord Jesus'.

A book about Queen Elizabeth II entitled *The Servant Queen and the King She Serves* was produced in celebration of her ninetieth year and of her being England's longest serving monarch. In it there are quotations from her writings and Christmas broadcasts in which she speaks of her Christian faith. Among the many wonderful things she has said about her trust in Jesus are these words which formed the conclusion to her 2011 Christmas Day Message to the Commonwealth.

The Christmas message shows us that God's love is for everyone. There is no one beyond its reach. In the last verse of the beautiful carol, O Little Town of Bethlehem, there's a prayer:

O Holy Child of Bethlehem,
Descend to us we pray
Cast out our sin
And enter in,
Be born in us today.

It is my prayer on this Christmas Day we might find
Room in our lives for the message of the love of God
through Christ our Lord.[142]

A painting entitled '*The Light of the World*' by the English Victorian Pre-Raphaelite artist, Holman Hunt, presents this important step of initial commitment to become a follower of Jesus in another way. The painting depicts Jesus as the Light of the World with a lamp in his hand and he is knocking on a door which seems not to have been opened for quite some time since it is overgrown with weeds and brambles. The door, Holman Hunt explained, represents the way into every person's life. Jesus is knocking gently at the door hoping to gain entry.

One of the early viewers informed Holman Hunt that he had made a mistake because there was no handle on the door. Hunt replied that there was no mistake since there is only one handle and that is on the inside because Jesus is not a god who forces himself on people. He respects our free-will. He waits gently knocking until we reach that point where of our own free-will we welcome him in. Come in Jesus and be the Lord of my life! The first time we give Jesus that welcome is the all important time but it doesn't end there. It's a welcome that we need to go on giving again and again. We need to ensure that Jesus is resident in our lives every single day. It's a like a marriage vow. The first time we say, 'I will' is the all important beginning but it's a commitment which married couples need to make to each other every day. The very first Christians used frequently to utter the Aramaic word 'Maranatha'. It is a very simple prayer which translates 'Lord come'! and they would have said it often throughout the day.

The journey of a life-time

Giving and speaking a serious heartfelt 'yes' to Jesus and inviting him to be central in our lives marks the start of the Christian journey. It is set to continue for the rest of our days after which it will be transformed into something altogether perfect beyond the grave. As with all journeys essential resources are needed to sustain us along the way. The most essential ones are trusting, witnessing and belonging.

Trusting

A Chinese laundry posted a notice in their front window which read, 'What we say we will do, we will do'! Having once become a committed follower of Jesus we have to begin to trust that what Jesus 'says in his word that he would do, he will indeed do'. This is why it is particularly important to read the gospels of Matthew, Mark, Luke and John because in so doing we can learn what Jesus offers us. For example he said, 'I am the bread of life. He who comes to me will never grow hungry, and he who believes in me will never grow thirsty'.[143] In other words Jesus promises to satisfy our deepest spiritual and emotional longings. Again Jesus promised, 'I am the Light of the World. He who believes in me will never walk in darkness, but have the light of life'.[144] In this instance Jesus is promising to dispel

---

[143] John 6:35
[144] John 8:12

the mental and moral confusion (darkness) that sometimes takes root in our minds.

To believe something is to mentally assent to it. To trust is one step beyond belief. For example there are many people in the world who believe that Jesus was a very great teacher and even that he rose again from the dead but that isn't the same as trusting in him. To trust someone is to rely on them. The Protestant reformer, Martin Luther, once wrote that there are two kinds of faith, 'historic faith' and 'true faith'. 'Historic faith' is intellectual assent to the facts but 'true faith' commits itself to the facts. Believing a surgeon can remove a tumour is mental assent but actually submitting to the surgeon and having an operation to remove the tumour is 'true faith'. In fact the Greek word 'pistis' which is translated faith means 'active trust'. Throughout the Christian journey we have to go on trusting that the Lord is always there with us, rooting for us, sustaining us and caring for us even in the hard times when there is pain and a seeming uphill climb. It is of course easier to feel that the Lord is with us when our outward circumstances are prospering. It takes a greater degree of trust and indeed added willpower when there is suffering or pain in our lives.

Knowing Jesus more fully

The better we know a good person the more likely we are to trust them. Jesus is no different, the more fully we know him the greater we will feel able to trust him. There are two things that will enable us to know Jesus more deeply. They are to study his life and teaching which we can find in the New Testament and to speak to him whenever we can.

As we read the gospels we get to know what Jesus is like. We see his compassion as he fed the hungry crowds. We witness his loving care as he healed the sick and cleansed the lepers. We recognise that he stood up for what was right and just and that he challenged those who mistreated the poor. Jesus was clear that if we are his followers we need to fill our minds with the things that he taught. To the people who believed in him he said, 'If you hold to my teaching, you are really my disciples'.[145] In his 'Sermon on the Mount' he urged the disciples to be both 'hearers and doers of his word'.

The Bible is more than just an ordinary book because the Lord can speak to us through its pages. John Wesley, the great revivalist preacher in eighteenth century England, listened to someone reading an introduction to St Paul's *Letter to the Romans* in a little chapel in the city of London on the 24th May, 1738. As he did so he said, 'I felt my heart strangely warmed, I felt I did trust in Christ alone and an assurance was given me that he had taken away my sins, even mine, and saved from the law of sin and death'. It is because the Bible is such a uniquely precious book that when a King or Queen of Great Britain is crowned they are presented with a copy by the Archbishop with the words, 'We present you with this Book, the most valuable thing this world affords. Here is wisdom. This is the Royal Law. These are the lively oracles of God'. There is a wonderful collect in the Church of England *Book of Common Prayer* which prays:

> Blessed Lord, who hast caused all holy Scriptures to be written for our learning; Grant that we may in such wise hear them, read, mark, learn and inwardly digest them, that by patience, and comfort of thy holy Word, we may embrace and ever hold fast the blessed hope of everlasting life, which thou hast given us in our Saviour Jesus Christ. Amen.

Reading books of Christian devotion and the biographies of great Christian men and women can significantly strengthen our faith in Jesus as can saying one of the great Christian creeds in a church service or even perhaps on our own in private. When we regularly

---

[145] John 8:31

repeat something of great truth it gradually becomes a part of us and deepens and increases our commitment. This is particularly true of the Apostles' Creed which dates back to the earliest Christian times and spells out the most important Christian beliefs. The early Christians spoke out Creeds as a way of strengthening their faith. It was also their declaration of faith to the pagan ruling Roman authorities.

Praying

Probably everyone in the world has at some time in their life cried out in prayer in a moment of desperation or sadness. But having become a committed follower of Jesus we now know that we need to direct our prayers to him. Prayer is simply communicating with the Lord. It's actually a two-way affair. We speak to Jesus our Lord and when we have done so we need to take a few moments and try to listen in the quiet of our inner being. Sometimes we will find ourselves aware of a gentle inner voice perhaps comforting us or prompting us to take a particular course of action. Jesus recommended finding a quiet place, perhaps our own room if we have one, and praying on our own. That said we can and should pray anywhere at any time and we should also pray together with other people. There is no one set right way to pray. It is best to communicate with the Lord in whatever way seems most natural. It's clear from the New Testament that Jesus prayed out aloud with an audible voice because the disciples remembered him doing so and some of his prayers are recorded in the gospels. Jesus also prayed silently. Anytime we are focusing on Jesus in our mind and thoughts or in our spirits we are communicating with him in prayer. Our longings, intentions and even our wandering thoughts and visions for the future can be forms of prayer.

It is important to ensure that our prayers are not solely focused on ourselves and our own needs. Indeed the majority of the prayers which are recorded in the New Testament are requests for the needs of other people. As well as praying for ourselves and for others it is a good to come to the Lord with thankfulness for the good things that make up our lives. The Greek word which means 'to give thanks' is 'eucharisto' and the Greek word for 'grace' is 'charis'. They are from the same root, as is the case in the English language, where to say grace means to give thanks. So to be thankful is to be in the grace of God. The apostle Paul wrote in his *Letter to the Philippians*, 'Don't be anxious about anything, but in everything, by prayer and petition, with *thanksgiving*, present your requests to God'.[146] It is also vital that whenever we do something wrong or hurtful we should immediately confess it and ask Jesus to forgive us, enable us to put it behind us, make amends and help us not to repeat it. The Apostle John reminds us at the beginning of his first letter that 'if we confess our sins, Jesus is faithful and just and will forgive us our sins and purify us from all unrighteousness'.[147]

When Jesus' disciples came and asked him to teach them to pray he urged them to keep praying for his Holy Spirit's presence to come to them.[148] This is very important because, as we saw in the earlier chapters, as Jesus' spirit fills our lives we grow in love, joy, peace, patience, kindness, goodness, faithfulness, gentleness and self-control. These qualities are described by the St Paul as 'the fruit of the Spirit' and clearly the more we grow in them the more like Jesus we will become. I have always loved the words that the bishop says in the Confirmation service in the old Church of England *Book of Common Prayer*. As he or she lays hands on the head of each person to be confirmed they pray 'Defend, O Lord, this thy servant that *he/she* may continue thine for ever; and daily increase in thy Holy Spirit more and

<hr>

146 Philippians 4:5
147 1 John 1:9
148 Luke 11: 13

more, until *he/she* come to thy everlasting kingdom'.

Jesus is the Good Shepherd and just as all good shepherds lead their sheep so he guides the lives of his followers. Asking for his wisdom and guidance in the major issues of our lives is therefore a very important aspect of our praying. The apostle James confidently asserted at the beginning of the letter he wrote that 'if any of you lacks wisdom, he should ask God, who gives generously to all without finding fault, and it will be given to him'.[149]

It can also be very helpful to have one or two well-known prayers written by others and make them our own by praying them to Jesus. Here are two such prayers but there are of course many others to choose from.

A Prayer of St Augustine (354-430)

O You, who are the light of the minds that know you,
the life of the souls that love you, and the strength of the
wills that serve you; help us so to know you that we
may truly love you; so to love you that we may fully
serve you, whom to serve is perfect freedom.

A Prayer of Richard, Bishop of Chichester (1197-1253).

Thanks be to you, our Lord Jesus Christ,
for all the benefits which you have given us,
for all the pains and insults which you have borne for us.
Most merciful Redeemer, Friend and Brother,
may we know you more clearly,
love you more dearly,
and follow you more nearly,
day by day.

---

[149] James 1:5

Belonging

John Donne, the seventeenth century poet and Dean of St Paul's Cathedral in London, wrote in a devotional piece that 'No man is an island entire of itself, every man is a piece of the continent, a part of the main'. These lines remind us that Jesus did not intend that his followers should go it alone. Robinson Crusoe Christians do not survive for long. Once we have become a follower of Jesus we need the support and encouragement of others. In his humanity during his earthly ministry Jesus found it necessary to have the support and encouragement of his disciples and the close friendship of Peter, James and John. There were others as we have already noted who befriended and encouraged him with their hospitality, friendship and resources.

What this means in practical terms is that if we are followers of Jesus we need to find and be part of a group of other Christian believers. Martin Luther once described the church as 'anywhere the people of God meet and the word of God is preached'. Luther also strongly urged the vital importance of this coming together with other Christians. He said on one occasion, 'When I am on my own in my house there is a coldness in my spirit but when I am in the great congregation a fire is kindled in my heart'. We should therefore try to meet with other believers, if possible once or twice each month and perhaps if we are able a little more frequently, to read and discuss Jesus' teachings, share concerns and pray together. We should also consider with Christian friends the best ways to make the Lord known and to bring his kingdom values to bear in our homes, places of work and our local neighbourhood.

We may find this support and encouragement that we need by going to a denominational or recognised institutional church and joining one of their home-based groups or we might decide to be part of a more informal gathering in someone's home or in our place of work. We must choose what ever option suits us best.

Witnessing

One thing we will doubtless be aware of is the importance of our home. Home and family are an integral part of the Christian tradition. From the very earliest times God dealt with people by families and households. His ancient people were commanded to keep the great Passover Festival by families in their homes. The New Testament speaks of the church as 'the household of God'. The English Puritan Christians in the reign of Queen Elizabeth 1 spoke of the home as 'the church in miniature'. This is why people rightly sometimes still say 'Christianity begins in the home'. If we share a residence with others or we have a family of our own we will obviously aim to live in a Christ-like way and be blessing and encouragement to them. If we have children we should do our best to bring them up so that they come to know the Lord for themselves and begin to live out his teaching in their lives.

The novelist, George Orwell , the author of *Nineteen Eighty Four*, wrote in his book *The Road to Wigan Pier*, 'We work because we have to and all work is done to provide us with leisure and the means of spending that leisure as enjoyably as possible'. Not all work as Orwell knew from his personal experience is pleasant, pleasurable or easy but Jesus never intended that our life's work should be a total 'daily grind'. Orwell's view can be contrasted to the findings of a visitor to a small village who went to pay a call on a great man of prayer who he had been told was a powerful influence in the neighbourhood. Eventually he found the man sitting in his shop. After a while the visitor asked, 'What service do you do for the Lord'? 'I mend shoes', the old man replied. 'Yes of course', replied the visitor, 'I realise how you earn your living but what do you do for the Lord'? 'I mend shoes', he replied. The old gentleman understood something very profound and that is our daily word should be a calling and something that we pray about and find the Lord's presence in.

Everyone of us has particular gifts and abilities and part of our Christian calling is to find work where we can best use them and serve others. Obviously we try if we can to find a job that brings us fulfilment and satisfaction but there will inevitably be periods in our lives when that simply may not be possible. Indeed if we are followers of Jesus we recognise that ultimately we work for him. The apostle Paul wrote, 'Whatever you do, work at it with all your heart, as working for the Lord, not for men, since you know that you will receive an inheritance from the Lord as a reward. It is the Lord Christ you are serving'.[150] Whatever else we do we can carry Christ's presence into our work place and seek to be good colleagues. Often our best witness in the work place is to do our work to a high standard and help others if time and opportunity arise. As St Francis of Assisi once said, 'Preach the gospel and if necessary use words'. The poet and Church of England clergyman, John Keble, wrote similarly that even in the very ordinary and domestic tasks we can find and reflect the presence of Jesus.

> If on our course our mind
> be set to hallow all we find
> new treasures still of countless price,
> God will provided for sacrifice.
>
> The trivial round, the common task
> will furnish all we need to ask,
> room to deny ourselves a road
> to bring us daily nearer God.

---

[150] Colossians 3:23

Perhaps all that has been said in this short chapter can be summed by saying that the purpose of becoming a follower of Jesus is to know him and make him known.

BIBLIOGRAPHY

Augustine, *City of God* (J. M. Dent and Sons Ltd, 1942)

Augustine, *The Confessions of Augustine* (Airmont Publishing Co, 1969)

Baker, H., *There is Always Enough* (Sovereign World, 2001)

Barclay, W., *The Gospel of Mark* (St Andrew Press, 1965)

Baxter, R., *Saints Everlasting Rest* (Marshallaton, 1824 facsimile edition)

Book of Common Prayer (Oxford University Press)

Bray, B., *The King's Son* (Bible Christian Book Room, 1902)

Bromiley, G. W, *Historical Theology an Introduction* (T and T Clark, 1978)

Bunyan, J., *The Pilgrim's Progress* (Penguin Books, 1965)

Dickens, C., *The Life of Our Lord* (World Books, 1934)

Franklin, B., *Autobiography and Other Essays* (OUP, 1993)

Graham, B., *Hope for Each Day* (Thomas Nelson, 2012)

Green, M., and Butcher, C., *The Servant Queen and the King she Serves* (Bible Society, 2016)

Hinn, B., *Good Morning Holy Spirit* (Nashville, 2004).

Hogg, Q., *The Door Wherein I Entered* (Collins, 1975)

Jobe, J., *Ecce Homo* (Harper Row, 1962)

Josephus, F., *Antiquities of the Jews* (Wilder Publications, 2018)

Langworth, R.C., Editor, *Churchill by Himself* (Ebury Press, 2008)

Larson, T., Editor, *Biographical Dictionary of Evangelicals* (IVP, 2003)

Lewis, C.S., *Mere Christianity* (Fontana Books, 1956)

Lewis, C.S., *The Problem of Pain* (Fontana, 1965)

Martin, H., Editor, *Selections for the Journal of John Wesley* (Epworth Press, 1960)

McGrath, A., *A Brief History of Heaven* (Blackwell, 2003)

Mitford, J., *The American Way of Death* (Penguin Books, 1995)

Muggeridge, M., *Jesus Rediscovered* (Fontana, 1972)

Nolland, L., *A Victorian Feminist Christian* (Paternoster, 2004)

Orwell, G., *Road to Wigan Pier* (Penguin Books, 1967)

Ramsay, M., *Be Still and Know* (Fount, 1982)

Russell, B., *Why I am not a Christian* (Simon and Schuster, 1957)

Telford, J., *Life of John Wesley* (Epworth Press, 1960)

DISCUSSION QUESTIONS AND TOPICS

Chapter 1 A Founder with universal appeal

In what ways do you see Jesus having universal appeal?

Discuss some of the major ways Jesus has impacted culture and society.

In what ways is Jesus good news to the poor?

Chapter 2 A Teaching for everyone

Why are Jesus' teachings valued across the globe even by those who are not practising Christians?

What can we learn from Jesus' teaching methods?

What does Jesus teach about himself?

Chapter 3 A life-changing experience

Why is forgiveness so important?

How does Jesus enable us to be forgiven and to forgive others?

Mother Teresa of Calcutta said, 'We can do no great things, only small things with great love'. What might this mean for us in practical every-day things?

Chapter 4 An exemplary leader to follow

Why is Jesus such an effective leader?

What aspects of Jesus' leadership would you like to see in your home, workplace, church, or your local community?

Share your experience of any leader who has helped, inspired, or encouraged you.

Chapter 5 A present help in suffering

Why do people who don't believe in God still blame him for the suffering in the world?

Good can sometimes come out of suffering. Share any examples of this either from general knowledge or from your own experience.

In what ways can Jesus' presence sustain us in times of pain, suffering or sickness?

Chapter 6 A way through death

Why do so many people live in fear of death?

What does Jesus teach us about death and how to overcome it?

How can we live as people of hope in today's world?

Chapter 7 A future hope

What reasons might make us believe there is a coming day of Judgement?

What do you think the life of heaven is like?

Read Revelation chapter 21: 1-8 and 22:1-6. What glimpses of heaven do we find particularly appealing?

Chapter 8 A straightforward faith

If someone asked us, 'What is a real Christian'? What answer would we give?

In the Gospel of John chapter 15:1-7 Jesus urges us to 'remain in him'. Share some of the ways which will help us to remain in his presence.

Write a short prayer asking Jesus to be present in your life or in a particular issue. If the opportunity arises, and you feel comfortable doing so, perhaps you could read it out.